West End Brat

The Montana Series

Book 2

N.M. McGregor

Published by Nadine Jolly, 2017
Printed in Canada

ISBN: 978-0-9958974-4-1

Published by Nadine Jolly

https://www.nmmcgregor.com
https://www.facebook.com/N.M.McGregorauthor/i
nbox/?s elected_item_id=238320410004489
https://twitter.com/NadineAuthor
https://www.instagram.com/n.m.mcgregor

Chapter 1

I stood with my hands covered in blood as my eyes traveled around the dark space. I was surrounded by concrete. I could see that much, but as to where I was, who knew. Suddenly, a single hanging light bulb flickered on. My mouth opened in a scream but there was no sound.

I was surrounded by dead bodies, women's bodies. They were strewn about like forgotten dolls. My curiosity overcame my horror. I turned over the nearest body. It was a young woman my age...a teenager. I didn't recognize her but her eyes looked familiar.

Each body I turned over had the same eyes, hauntingly familiar but I couldn't put my finger on it. I came to the last body. When I turned her over I saw that it was me, and my empty lifeless eyes stared back at me. I realized then that the bodies were all different but they all had my eyes.

My blossoming into womanhood, which began on Friday night, abruptly ended with my need to go home on Sunday and get things ready for the week. After all, I still had three brothers to look out for. They were all older than me (Alex by only four minutes but still), and primarily concerned for my welfare, so I owed it to them to make an appearance. We'd all aged prematurely after dad's death so in some ways it was a relief for them when Danny's artistic partner Adam took me under his wing. At least it had been a relief since it had always been platonic up until now....

Adam and I left "the mansion." That was my nickname for his apartment above his parents' garage. Their house was the real mansion, situated as it was in beautiful Shaughnessy, Vancouver. While he drove his sexy black 280Z I reflected on our amazing weekend on the quick drive home....

His body, the things he did to me...awakening sensations I never knew existed, feeling things deep within, primal things I never dreamed possible.

When we arrived at my place he opened the door for me, ever the gentleman, and pulled me into an embrace and deep kiss that had my belly doing gymnastics.

Adam would pick me up after band practice the next day, the time between now and then was torturous. *How could I possibly last without those lips on mine?* I sighed as I entered the house. Everyone was home: Danny was in the kitchen doing the dishes, Alex was at the kitchen table doing his homework and Ace had just sat down to look over a paper that was due the next day.

They all looked up when I casually strolled in with an ear splitting grin.

"Hi guys, it's great to be home," I said, with a back cracking stretch and a yawn that made my eyes all glassy. Nothing was said but they all looked at me the same way. They looked amusing so I laughed and sauntered to the kitchen for some Evian water and a cup of coffee.

As I sat I gave off another contented sigh and stretched out my legs. I surveyed my three brothers... who had still not said a word and all still wore the same expression.

Danny sat down opposite me in the kitchen while Alex and Ace went back to their individual tasks. Dan's look was discerning and in a flash I knew what he saw. His sister changed from a girl to a woman. In a flash I shifted from a contented, self-amused Mona Lisa to a blushing teenager.

"I've got homework," I mumbled, getting up and heading to my room. I closed the door, and flopped down on my bed. I grinned, replaying the images of us in Adam's bedroom…in the kitchen…in the shower, on the couch, on the floor... My body was all a-tingle when there was a knock on my door.

"Montana, can I come in?" Danny asked.

"Sure bro, come on in."

"I was just wondering how your weekend was?"

He was watching me, his gaze relaxed, his body anything but…. He reminded me of a cat ready to spring.

"Mmm ... I had amazing sex with the man I am in love with and will one day marry," I answered, suddenly grinning again. I couldn't seem to help the grinning thing. I felt incredible and my bones and muscles felt like mush. "And it was totally amazing," I gushed.

Danny just sat there with his mouth hanging open. "You asked," I answered in my own defence.

"Montana, has Ace ever had the protection conversation with you? I mean, I am a guy and I've done with girls what you just did with my best friend, but you're my little sister and I'm not sure what to say to you. Part of me wants to know the details and the other part wants to phone Adam and then go and punch him in the nose."

I sat up. "The protection conversation, do you mean did we use condoms?"

He nodded vigorously, "Yes that is precisely what I mean," Danny answered.

"Of course, Dan. Think about it, this is Adam we're talking about here. He's not just any guy and despite what I know or don't know, he would have taken everything into consideration and played out ten different options before deciding on the method he chose."

"You're right he isn't just any guy, he's a man, and you're still a teenager so I'm telling you right now that I hope you guys are being smart about this."

I was so embarrassed; I couldn't believe I was having this conversation with my older brother. But, our parents were dead, my mom since I was little, so unless I wanted to talk to our oldest brother Ace, who was very overprotective, Dan would have to do.

"Dan, I haven't had *the* conversation with Ace or more accurately, he has never had it with me. And to tell you the truth I don't think either of us could handle that conversation," I said with a laugh. "Maybe *you* could have it with me," I said giving him a no nonsense look. "I totally trust Adam with this but I should know how the protection aspect works on both sides, and all my options."

He sighed, "Okay I'll tell you everything you want to know but first tell me, are you okay?"

"Geez Danny, would you give me a break? I'm fine. Great actually, who am I kidding?" I said with a giggle, "I am doing amazing. I never thought it would be so invasive. I feel like every part of me has changed. I was completely gone in the process, just a bundle of sensations. I never thought about anything — it was so cool." I paused for a moment before asking, "Do you think Ace knows?"

"I'm sure he does," Danny answered.

"I've spent the night there before and you guys never suspected anything. So why now?"

"Well you look different. Have you looked in a

mirror? You're glowing. You look really beautiful actually, a dead giveaway that something big has happened," he said, with a small grin.

"Ha." I sat up and looked in the mirror. I did look different, but I couldn't see the glowing thing that Danny described. Artists. I sat back down on my bed. "I don't see what you see but that's okay. I do know quite a bit, you know. I have a lot of older friends. I really wanted to share my experience with someone I trust, and to be honest, Eddy was the first person I thought of. He has always been there for me as a friend and protector and he doesn't judge. He just listens...."

Eddy's our family friend, he grew up with us in our hood and was closer in age to Danny than me but we had always been buds. Eddy had always been great at keeping his friendships within our family individual so as not to create bad feelings with any one of us. He hung out with Alex and me at beach parties and with Danny and their other pals, and played a lot of football with Ace. He was our friend, and the only person we knew who we all liked equally.

Danny gave me a searching look and seemed to come to some sort of conclusion about something. "Mo, you can tell me anything," he sighed. "There was a time when you couldn't have told me anything. I wouldn't have been able to handle it. You can tell Eddy if it makes you more comfortable. I know he has been there for you in ways I never have. But right now, I am here and you can share with me as your confidant with no repercussions. I swear, I will just listen and ooh and ahh at the right parts." He said this with a laugh.

I decided to take a chance with my bro, Dan the Man.... I realized he'd just taken a huge chance and reached out to me. That was probably the biggest speech I'd ever heard him give. Our friendship had grown just before dad's death, with Adam and I dating and the three of us being together on many adventures. And since, we had grown even closer. So, for the following hour I spoke of everything

Adam-related from the last two years, from my perspective as a girl —not his sister.

I began my story two years previous when Adam, a complete stranger to me at that time, had driven me home from a movie. Dan knew this part, but he didn't know of the slow seduction on Adam's part. I told him about the book on the seat between us and how it had been open to a poem that had caught my eye. I spoke of our instant connection, and our first serious conversation after the Halloween dance at the beach party.

I shared Adam's observations on Mercy, my nemesis, and his warning about her regarding my safety. All my big brothers looked out for me, although Alex, my twin, hadn't really grown up until recently.

At many parts, Dan's eyes grew big but he kept his promise, oohing and ahhing like a best buddy. I think he gained a new perspective on me as a person, not just a family member. I told him all the details of the weekend, how it started, the things

Adam did and how they made me feel. I admit I told him things I probably wouldn't have told anyone else but I was testing Dan's resolve with the last bit. I wanted to make sure he was the real deal in his role as confidant. He raised his eyebrows a few times, but my frank language didn't throw him and he was respectful and controlled himself until I was finished.

We spent another hour or so together during which he asked me questions and from there we rolled into the birth control options. Then, he answered some of my questions about pregnancy and how my birth control options would keep me safe. I was impressed. He'd clearly done some homework.

At the end of our conversation, I gave him a big hug of thanks for listening like he did instead of cutting me off or judging me without any consideration for my perspective. Most guys could be blockheads at times, but Dan was an artist and he and I shared some similar qualities.

Dan had never really been against me. He was almost always on my side in debates. Particularly when my oldest brother Ace was involved. Ace often wore blinders when it came to me. He knew that Ace could be much harder on Alex and me than our dad ever was, so Danny felt he owed it to Alex and me to lean on the side of fairness in all things. Still, it was a big leap of trust for me and I felt it had been the right thing to do.

At school the next day I told my best girlfriend Chrissie about my weekend and how I had shared it with Danny when I got home.

"Wow Mo, that is really wild. Was Danny okay with it?" Chrissie asked, with a bit of awe in her voice.

"He seemed to be," I said, "but he will be seeing Adam at art school today so I'm hoping he doesn't backslide into my 'big brother' and start a fight or anything." I grinned. I didn't really think that would happen. I felt, somehow, that all the family relationships with Adam would be okay.

Alex walked by us and gave us a wink on his way to his next class. He was so tall now he had surpassed Danny and was just shy of Ace's height, but where Ace was hugely built as a football player should be, Alex was a gangly 16 year old. He had muscle but he was ultra-lean with very little body fat. Chrissie watched him walk by and sighed.

"Chrissie, why don't you just tell Alex you want to be with him?" I huffed.

Chrissie had been in love with Alex since the third grade when she and I became best friends. Chrissie and Alex had gone out for almost a year but Alex's success with the band had become too much for her and she couldn't come to terms with the groupies and popularity. She wanted a quiet intimate relationship. She answered with a sigh.

School that day seemed to take forever. As soon as it ended, I was out the door and home in a flash. I did my chores before band practice and by the time Alex and Otter arrived I was ready to go.

"Gee Montana, in a bit of a rush?" Alex asked, smiling.

"Yeah," I said, sticking out my tongue at him, pretending to be annoyed.

Knowing Adam's appearance was imminent had me in a great mood and practice was super easy. Such was not always the case. After my ex-boyfriend Ralph's death and my father's death, things had been rough between Alex and me for a bit. I knew now that neither death would ever be forgotten, but I was no longer being controlled by my grief and this weekend had done a lot to restore me. Pretty amazing how when life gets good it's easier to forgive and move on.

We played for two hours and then took a break to discuss the gig we had coming up that weekend. As we were wrapping up Adam showed and took me back to his place. Privacy and intimacy were the only things on my mind....

"Adam, I thought today would never end. All I

wanted was to see your face and, well, the rest of you," I finished with a sly grin.

"Me too," he said, as he leaned over and kissed me with barely restrained hunger. "Do you have homework?"

I was going to say 'none of your damn business,' but instead I smiled sweetly as we pulled up to the mansion. I answered that I had finished before band practice. Once inside, I watched him unpack his own school-related work from his bag in front of a large window. As he leaned over his easel, the sun decided to peep out from behind the clouds and create a halo around him.

"Don't move," I said, as I grabbed his camera off the bar and started snapping pictures. A small grin appeared but other than that he did as I asked.

"By the way, did Dan say anything to you today?"

"About?" His eyebrows drew slightly together and then the tension evaporated as he saw my easy manner.

"We had a talk last night-- the protection talk," I said, with a smirk. Adam blushed furiously.

"He was just checking that we were being smart, and of course I said 'duh.' Adam knows what he is doing. But then I did have a few questions, so we talked for a while. It was really good for me and I hoped it wouldn't cause any weirdness for you two."

He shook his head no. Although sometimes Adam seemed more sensitive than I was about things, he had always said he appreciated my candor. He was also always making me look words up. Leaving his halo behind, he made his way over and kissed me with a longer, hungrier kiss than the first. I slid in tight and wrapped my legs around his hips. He picked me up and carried me to his *bedroom.*

I arrived home around eleven that evening to find Ace at the kitchen table studying for an exam.

Ace looked up and smiled when he saw me. I joined him at the table and we chatted about the weather and school for a while. It wasn't until I stood up to get ready for bed that Ace finally spoke his mind.

"I haven't seen you for a few days, Peanut. Where have you been spending all your time?" I was annoyed by his question as he knew perfectly well where I had been spending my time. I chose to be rosy and answered that I had been with Adam.

He smiled, "I know. I guess what I really want to know is if you're keeping yourself together?" He reached out and grabbed my hand, giving it a gentle squeeze of encouragement.

"It's all good chief." He smiled at my use of my pet name for him. "I am tired, and boy, do I need to sleep." He hugged me goodnight and I slept like the dead.

After that night the same pattern continued until Friday, which was gig night. Instead of practice after school, Alex, Otter, and I loaded all our equipment into Eddy's car and took it down to the *Dover Arms* on Denman Street where we were playing that night. We set everything up – amp for guitar and bass, my drums -- and did our sound checks right away so we could go home and take our time getting ready to play later that night.

I showered and cleaned up and put on a pair of black jeans that molded to my body and a white tank top. The guys were dressed all in black. Our first set went off without a hitch and was received by an enthusiastic crowd. The Dover was a dimly lit pub with a fairly large seating section.

Ace, 'his woman' Kristine, Danny, and Adam were at a table in the back corner. On the break I left the band guys talking to our adoring fans. Female groupies would be more accurate. I headed over to the table in the back.

The doorman stopped me on the way. "Hey," he said, "you are really good. How long have you been playing?" We stood for a moment while I politely answered his questions. He informed me that he also played and asked if I would take a look at his kit which was in the back. I looked at Adam, who seemed busy in heated conversation, rolled my eyes at the doorman and followed him backstage.

"Where are they?" I asked, as I looked around and saw nothing resembling a drum kit. He grabbed me and twisted my arm behind my back and leaned in to kiss me.

"Hey!" I yelled. "Get your goddamn hands off me. What the hell do you think you are you doing?"

"Shut up little girl while I *do you* right here."

He was a big guy, almost as big as Ace, and he had an iron grip on my wrists. I panicked and started to squirm. As I opened my mouth to scream I heard a voice say, "Hey James, what are you doing with my sister?"

James stopped and looked up at Alex's voice. "She's your sister?"

"Yeah, and I don't take kindly to anyone messing with her either. So, let her go and we'll be cool, okay?" And just like that, he let me go and I walked as cool as I could over to Alex on very shaky legs. "Montana, why don't you go have a drink with Ace and Adam while James and I have a quick word." Alex spoke but never looked at me, his gaze never left James.

This was a new Alex, one I had never really seen before. His eyes glittered dangerously and although James was much heavier than Alex he looked unsure of himself. Alex was like a dangerous cat, slim, quick and deadly.

I left and all but ran to the table where the guys and Kristine were sitting. I felt totally shaken up. That guy was going to rape me and I couldn't have done a thing about it. Adam asked me if I was okay, and as I wasn't ready to discuss it with him, I just nodded my head and took a big swig from his beer.

Alex came out a few minutes later and gave me a glance that spoke all I needed to know. All was well. I breathed a sigh of relief. On the way back up to the stage he paused in the stairwell, put his arm on my shoulder and asked me how I was doing.

"Honestly, that freaked me out-- but yeah, I'll be fine. Also, I am some kind of pissed. Who does that motherfucker think he is anyway? I know now why you gave me all those warnings a year ago when we started all this. I should have known better, but he said he wanted me to take a look at his drums. Alex, he was going to rape me right there behind the stage and I was helpless to do anything about it," I choked out the last bit as the tears finally welled up.

"Hey Montana, it's okay. It's not your fault. I've been doing this for a long time and believe me, you're not the first James has tried that with, which is why I followed you guys." As Alex spoke, I choked back my tears and focused on what I needed to do with the band. Only my twin could know how I was feeling and reassure me so quickly.

"Thanks Alex...for watching out for me. I'll be more careful next time," I said, with conviction.

The incident put behind us, we finished up the last set and, as it was Friday night, I went home with Adam to spend the weekend.

"Adam, do you have any rum? I am needing something with a bit more kick than wine at the moment."

He frowned at me but said he would check. He came back with a generous rum and coke for me and poured the wine from my glass to his....I twisted the lime he had so thoughtfully provided and took a big swig of the Cuba Libre, sighed, and finally felt my shoulders drop and relax for the first time that night.

"We're alone now Montana. Want to tell me what is going on? I know you can fool Ace and Danny from time to time, but you have never fooled me. I saw that exchange between you and Alex after your first set. What on earth...?"

"Okay. I will tell you, Adam, but please don't be mad at me." I hated it when anyone was mad at me because it made me feel as though I had let them down in some way. I told him what happened. His response was rather surprising. One I had not as yet seen, nor would see often in the future. For the first time I saw Adam's eyes change colour as they went almost black. It was the equivalent to Danny's jaw twitching and Ace's *look* which meant they were furious. I was curious as to his thoughts. I knew he wasn't angry with me. He probably wanted to go back to the club.

He didn't say a word, instead he went and stood looking out his bay window at the darkness. When he calmed down he gave me a speech about finding healthier outlets than booze to help with my stress. Inwardly, I smirked as I knew by the change in direction the storm had passed. I was not the one he was mad at....

"Adam, I appreciate everything you have said, just please, don't say anything to Dan, okay? He will get stressed out and tell Ace, and then my playing days will be over because he overreacts to everything that has to do with me."

He frowned as he said, "Montana I don't think that is a fair assessment of your brothers. Dan and Ace are here to protect you and watch out for you and help you out when you need it. Keeping this kind of secret from them is a mistake, especially if they hear about this from someone else. Then they will be furious and make you quit. You need to be mature about this and be honest with them."

I said nothing. I thought many things and my first thought was to tell him to shove it. Why did his advice piss me off so much? I didn't know but I would have to figure it out. I didn't like ultimatums that was for sure. Adam's voice broke through my thoughts, "If you don't, I will tell them anyway because I don't want to hold on to this type of secret when they have the right to know. You tell them or I tell them,. Okay?"

I sighed in agreement but I wasn't happy about it. We went to bed and the next morning Adam drove me to the house and came in with me to make sure I told the whole truth about the previous night. The guys were at the kitchen table. All except Alex, who was still in bed.

"Hey guys, what's up?" Danny asked, with a small frown of concern.

"Montana has something to tell you about last night." Adam started. I looked from one to the other and told them my tale and included my conversation with Adam. When I was done, all were silent. The seconds felt like minutes as Adam and I waited for a response.

Finally, Danny spoke up. "Montana, this is serious stuff, are you okay?" I nodded. "Do you still want to play tonight?"

"Of course I want to play!" I was trying to keep the exasperation out of my voice, "This is what I do, this is who I am. More than anything I want to play. Don't let one little hiccup screw things for me, please. I have come too far and felt too much."

"Then, I will go and keep my eye on you. I think

we will have to make sure that one of us is on watch at all times," Danny finished.

"I appreciate your offer, but it was only one isolated incident. After all this time what are the chances of it happening two nights in a row?"

The guys exchanged looks.…"It only takes once...." Ace finally said. He seemed unnaturally calm. Usually he was freaking out and ordering me around. "Now that this has happened I don't want you going anywhere by yourself when you're in the clubs, okay? And we will watch it for a while and see what happens." They were looking so serious so I gave the guys a hug. Adam and I headed out for a walk to do some photography. Once out the door I gave Adam a big hug also and thanked him for making me fess up. Then I stuck out my tongue and he called me a brat as he chased me down the path to the beach. When he caught me we fell into the soft sand and he kissed me for a long time.

One of the great things about living in the West End of Vancouver was being able to walk from our place to a strip filled with shops and restaurants and then, barely a stone's throw further be at English Bay. In fact, Ace probably could throw a stone from our place to the beach but it would likely hit somebody on the way down. Go left or right and you lost the crowds. To the right was the way into a huge amazing park, named after one of Canada's Governor Generals and the patron saint of hockey. Lord Stanley. Why did I know this? I had to study him for one of my exams.

We headed to Stanley Park and took pictures for a few hours, capturing life and things that inspired us. He walked me home early then headed off to do some errands before coming to the show that night.

When I entered the house Alex was busy in the kitchen. I sat down and talked while he cooked. I shared how the morning's conversation had gone with Ace and Danny. Frankly, he was relieved.

"Good," he said. "I told you I didn't want to play bodyguard. I have to fight the groupies off me and having to look out for you too doesn't exactly turn me on."

"Do you think I need to worry at the club tonight?" I asked, hesitant. Despite my desire to play, as the day turned to early night I began to feel anxious about any further confrontation with the massive James.

"Eddy will be staying for the show tonight and James knows his reputation. So, I seriously doubt it unless James has a death wish."

We ate and got ready for the show; Eddy drove us and stayed at the stage while we did our sound check.

"Montana, I'm official bodyguard tonight and I'm keeping my eye on you. If you're out of my sight for more than 10 seconds I'll come looking for you," Eddy said.

I nodded and smiled in relief. Eddy was more than capable of doing the job, probably better than anyone I knew. Eddy wanted to be a cop and he was very observant, very strong and had great instincts.

Danny and Adam arrived and waved just as we were going on stage. I noticed they sat at a table where they had a good view of James. The first set went off without a hitch. I was being checked out but that was not unusual.

On the break I went to the washroom letting Otter know as I went by. Alex was being held up by his groupies. I was just finishing up and about to leave when a big guy entered the bathroom and asked me if I was Montana. "No," was my answer, as I attempted to walk around the guy and back out into the club.

"Yes you are," he said, as he grabbed my arm and twisted it behind my back and propelled me behind the stage and towards the back door. He was just opening the door to push me out when who should walk out from behind the stage, but Adam.

"Where do you think you're going with my girlfriend?" he asked.

For a big guy he was fast. He twisted my arm

higher so he could free his other hand to swing at Adam, but he wasn't fast enough and Adam grabbed the guy's fist and pushed him back against the doorframe. The guy tripped Adam and dragged me out the door again only to find Eddy standing there. One punch to the nose and the guy let me go.

Others had noticed the fight and the owner came back to see what was going on. It turned out the guy from the bathroom was an off duty bouncer. He had been paid by James to get me out of the club and into the alley.

Needless to say, both bouncers were fired and everything calmed down. The owner was terrified of us pressing charges. I left Adam to deal with that as he seemed to possess a legal verbiage that none of us had except Ace, but he wasn't there.

The owner was impressed by Eddy and asked him if he would be interested in filling in for the remainder of the night as doorman. Eddy agreed. They couldn't have picked a better guy. Danny came over to see if I was okay and I said yes but my arm hurt. To be honest, it felt like it was on fire but the last thing I wanted was more attention.

We finished the gig and packed up Eddy's car. I used one arm but nobody seemed to notice. Danny drove back to our place. We were unpacking in silence when Adam asked to look at my arm.

"I think it's broken, Mo. Dan come and take a look at this," Adam called. They moved it around a bit and when they turned it left, from the elbow down it really hurt. Understatement or what? My knees buckled and only the urge to throw up stopped me from fainting. Maybe it was all the blood draining from my face that gave Adam a clue.

"I'm taking you to emergency," Adam said.

"It's fine really, just a little sore, "I replied -- really not wanting to go to the hospital and sit in emergency all night just to be told it was a sprain.

Adam made a call from our house before we left and when we arrived at the hospital I was taken immediately into the x-ray room. Wow, nice to have

31

some pull. Obviously, Adam had called in a favour at the hospital to which his parents were huge financial contributors.

And as usual, Adam was right. It was broken. Not a bad break, so two weeks with a cast should mend it pretty good I was told. I asked if I could play drums and the doctor laughed and told me if I could stand the pain and play with a cast on, then go ahead.

Adam had offered me a drink at the club as I had been looking pale but I had declined. I told him I would take that drink now. So after dropping off Eddy's car back at the club we stopped in at 7-11 to get some coke to go with our stash of rum at the house. When we made it back, Ace was home and asked what happened.

Danny, Adam, Alex and I all took turns in the narrative explaining what had happened and the results. When we were finished Ace said, "I was afraid of this happening Montana. Like I said last year, I think you should consider a new career."

I was stunned. I think we all were as the room went dead silent, except Alex who was muttering under his breath about told you so's….Finally, Dan spoke up, "Ace, what you are asking is unrealistic. That would be like asking you to give up football or your major in college. This is just as important to Montana. How could you ask her to simply throw in the towel when our parents always taught us to never give up on our dreams?"

Another silence as we all processed Dan's words. He was right of course. We all knew it, and Ace knew it. But we also knew that if he came to that conclusion on his own we could avoid a heated argument and he could save face.

"How about we compromise?" Ace finally said. "You can play once you're healed, just not at that bar."

I was going to argue but Adam squeezed my hand, 'not now' he seemed to say by the squeeze. Lose the fight and win the war. So instead I sighed and conceded that it was a wise choice, "But, I wish to add in a condition of my own."

Ace's eyebrows rose but he said nothing so I continued. "The band has a gig in 6 days. The doc said I could play the gig as long as I could play without pain. And, seeing as he is a friend of Adam's parents," I added, with a small smirk of victory, "*and* I totally trust him, and he is the best in his field, *that* should be good enough for everyone here."

I knew it was a brat move, but hey, I am what I am. Again the room went dead quiet as everyone knew I had won that round but no one was fool enough to point it out. Finally, Ace smiled a slow smile that showed he conceded that round to me. He reached over and tapped my cast. I kept a straight face even though I could feel the reverberations down to my toes.

"Okay, you can have your way as long as you rest and don't play until you have to."

After that we all sat back and relaxed with our

rum and cokes. The subject changed and everything was once again as it should be. Peaceful. It was late, so Adam decided to leave and thought it prudent for me to stay home, which made me pout on the inside but I stayed cool on the outside. I walked him to his car.

"I'll see you in the morning. We'll go for breakfast and then how about a walk up in the mountains?" "Yes, that sounds amazing," I replied. He chuckled as he got in his car. I stayed and waved until he was out of sight.

When I came back inside Ace wanted to talk to me. Everyone else had gone to bed so it was just the two of us. "Montana, are you really okay? What I mean… is any of this bringing up stuff from the past? You know, like creating a disturbance in your emotions… like what happened when Ralph died... when you broke down, and well, you know— forgot things?"

About a year before I had suffered a complete breakdown after Ralph had died. Then our dad had been killed in a work accident. His death had been right on the heels of Ralph's and that had affected Ace even more than me. "You must have been scared," he added.

"Yes, I was terrified. But unlike last time, I wasn't alone, and I wasn't trying to be alone in my torment. I knew Adam and the guys were there."

"That is fine for right now, maybe even another year or two…But in the near future, all of us will be done school and will be moving on with jobs and careers and there is no guarantee that someone will always be there for you, so what then?"

"I don't know the answer Ace. All I can say is, I guess I will slay that dragon when it presents itself. Besides," I added with a wink, "Adam isn't going anywhere. You watch, he will marry me and then he can hire me a body guard." We both laughed at that and went our separate ways and mine was to my bed. Exhaustion drew me into a deep sleep. Deep but troubled.

Someone wants to hurt me...

Chapter 2

I was backed into a corner. 5 sets of glowing eyes surrounded me, a red 6th set glittered as the voice spoke. "I have you now, Montana Stanford. Finally, no one is here to rescue your pathetic self."

"Who are you?" I asked red eyes.

"Your destiny. Your end. You have seen and heard too much, you cannot be allowed to live." Suddenly the glowing eyes became my eyes and the red eyes played a movie for my eyes alone. I saw what I did not want to see. I saw things buried in my subconscious and things to come. As soon as I'd seen something it would disappear. I struggled to remember and failed.

The last scene died out and before I could speak, the glowing red eyes returned to my eyes but the voice remained the same..."You shall die Montana Stanford, your silly brothers and your rich boyfriend can't save you from what is going to happen."

I screamed a long terrified scream.

"Montana, Mo. Wake up, it's only a nightmare. Mo."

I felt someone shaking me awake. "What happened?"

Alex replied, "I woke up shivering and then I heard you screaming." My spiritually connected brother had felt my fear even before I woke the house. Ace and Dan were next in, and Ace had a bat.

"It's okay," Alex said, "she was only having a nightmare."

"You good, Peanut?" Ace asked, tapping the bat against his hand. I looked around for any glowing eyes. When none appeared, I realized that whatever I had seen that was sending me a message wasn't here now and I was safe, for the moment anyway.

I nodded and we all went back to bed. It took a

long time for those glowing eyes to stop haunting me. Every time I was almost asleep they would appear before me -- and the voice -- I kept hearing the voice and just as I was finally falling into sleep I recognized it…. It belonged to Mercy. If ever a name was ironic. According to the dictionary mercy is "the kind or forgiving treatment of someone who could be treated harshly." Mercy sucked up kindness and forgiveness and spat out pure evil. Jealous, hateful...she was a complete bitch! Why did she have it in for me...? I wouldn't put up with her B.S., that's all. Who has the time?

I loved Sundays, breakfast out and fun! Who could ask for a better day than that! My arm was just a dull throb and emotionally I was fine, no repercussions. The red eyes had become a distant memory and I was able to shrug off the events of the last two nights.

As Adam and I sat having breakfast I listened to him discuss the travel plans that he and Danny had made for the summer. Since becoming best friends years ago, they had decided to travel to Europe the summer after they finished art school.

"Maybe the two of you will run into Katya," I said with a nasty grin. He grimaced, "Please don't remind me. She will go down in history as my biggest mistake of all time!"

I had to remind him. "You never did tell me how that situation played out with Katya. Did you end up sleeping with her on my living room rug?"

"Honestly, Mo. Do you really want to hear about Katya?" Katya was a girl who spent about a week with us last summer. She was from Paris and had intimidated me as she appeared to be the "perfect woman." Danny had met her when he was in Paris on a scholarship last winter and she had "spent some time" with Adam while she was here staying with us.

"I mean do you want to tell me about all the things you did with Ralph, or Matt, or would you prefer to keep that to yourself?" he asked in all

sincerity. I thought about that. Did I want to share?
Well, as far as Matt was concerned there was not a
lot to tell. Ralph was a different story but even so,
as Adam fully realized, I was a virgin so obviously I
had not much to tell of the sexual side of things. But
that is not exactly what he meant. He wanted to
know if I wanted to share intimate details, sex or
otherwise.

"Montana, those are your memories and I have
no right to pry into them. And the thing with Katya,
well, I think we both know I wasn't really on top of
that situation."

"Oh I beg to differ, Adam. You were soooo... on
top when I walked in the room," I responded with a
mischievous grin.

"Ace was right. You are such a brat," he said,
laughingly. I decided to let him off the hook for
now. My curiosity would have to settle for cuddles.

Alex and I stopped at the Muffin Break on our
way to school the next morning to get a coffee and a

muffin. The girl who served us was just getting off shift. She was new to our school that year and I didn't know her at all but I said hi. She was staring at Alex. He glanced over and said hi, she looked back at me and said; "Aren't you the Stanford twins?"

"Yes," I responded. She didn't take her eyes off Alex. What did she want, for me to set her up with him?

"So he is that cool guitar player I have seen playing around town."

Was she asking me or telling me? I rolled my eyes but said nothing.

"Wow," she said, "he is amazing."

Poor girl. She was smitten with him, like all the girls in our school. Feeling a bit sorry for her, I told her where we were playing on the weekend and gave her a free ticket to get in. Her eyes got big and she seemed thrilled as she thanked me.   I turned to see where Alex was so we could leave and found him talking to a few girls. When will it stop? And then I almost dropped my coffee. Alex, feeling my astonishment, looked up from his conversation to where I was staring. I felt rather than saw his look of astonishment match my own. What had drawn our attention was Ralph. Well, not really Ralph, but his twin stood before us. He looked up at me, then to Alex. And maybe it was my imagination, but suddenly all chatter in the Muffin Break ceased.

I know it's a cliché but you could have heard a pin drop. It was only a second and then noise and chatter returned to its regular volume. We said hi in unison, he smiled and said hi back.

"What's your name?" I asked.

"Tim, what's yours?" As I was about to respond, Alex stepped in and shook his hand and said he was Alex and I was Montana.

"Hmmm," he said, "the lead drummer and the lead singer for that kick ass band that everyone keeps talking about, Behind Blue Eyes?"

44

Alex smiled, "That's right," he answered.

"I play a little myself," Tim said.

"A little what?" Alex asked him. I felt my heart beat increase as I waited for the answer. Somehow I knew he would say drums…and he did. How uncanny and eerie I thought.

"Why don't you come by our place after school and jam with us?" Alex asked. Tim smiled and nodded his agreement. We told him to meet us out front after school and walk back to our place with us.

All day I had flashback memories of Ralph. This boy Tim had an uncanny resemblance to Ralph and not just his looks either. His mannerisms and his voice were the same, his height, the only thing completely different was the weight. Tim was broader than Ralph. And the eyes. Ralph's had been green and this guy's were blue. I was really curious to find out more about him after school. Who he was and where he came from, and why was he showing up now in our lives? Coincidence? I felt it wasn't a coincidence but I also could not think of any sinister reason as to why he was there.

The four of us met up after school. Otter did not seem overly friendly, which surprised me, but none of us questioned him and Tim didn't seem to notice. Nor did he seem to mind when Otter gave him the third degree.

"How come I haven't seen you around?" he asked.

"I dropped out of my last school when we moved here two months ago and I haven't registered here yet. I need to work, it's just my mom and me. She's on disability so I work to make up the difference."

"How old are you?" I asked.

"Sixteen," he responded.

"Same age as us. Hmm...." Otter seemed satisfied with the answer and didn't ask any more questions but he also didn't warm up to the guy either.

"Otter," I whispered to him as we fell a bit behind Tim and Alex. "What exactly is your problem with this guy?"

"There is something not right, Mo, I'm telling you this all seems fake somehow."

When we arrived at our house we grabbed some drinks and headed into the garage. I grabbed a chair for Tim and told him to have a seat while we made sure our equipment was ready and instruments tuned. When we were good to go, we played all our newer stuff including a song I had written for Ralph.

When we were done Tim leaped from his seat and enthusiastically said; "Holy crap, you guys really rock!" I grinned in response and invited him to try my drums. He didn't want to at first. He was shy. Man, did I know how that felt, and so I pulled a Ralph.

Using Ralph's kit that his mom had given me in his memory, I had Tim come up and follow my riffs. The first riff being the first one Ralph had taught me. This was so weird. Tim had training so it didn't take him long to figure things out. Then the guys joined in and we all played together. It was like magic. I felt the type of connection I had with Ralph when I first played on my new kit.

I had to excuse myself as all of a sudden I was feeling overwhelmed. Alex followed me into the kitchen a few minutes later to see if I was okay.

"You felt that amazing energy?"

"Yes, I felt it, and to be honest it scared me," I answered.

We talked about the uncanny resemblances and the brief talk brought me back to reality. I was ready to go back to rehearsal. For the next two hours I played riffs and he would copy and then we would all play together.

During our last song Danny and Adam showed up, and they had no game face at all when they saw Tim. Their mouths were hanging open and it was hard not to laugh at them. Like us, they must have questioned for a moment if they were seeing a ghost. Danny dropped his coke and Adam was frozen at his side. When we played the end of our song I introduced Adam and Danny to Tim. They appeared to be on autopilot as they took turns shaking his hand. As Tim was thanking us and getting ready to leave he noticed Adam's drawing on the wall of Alex, Ralph and me. Adam had made it for me after the funeral. Tim studied it for a moment and asked who the guy was.

"That," said Alex, "was my best friend and Montana's boyfriend. He taught her how to play and he died about a year ago."

Tim examined Ralph's likeness; he seemed to come to some conclusion and commented on his way out that he liked how Ralph was passing a drum stick in the photo. We waved bye and said, "See you tomorrow if you want to play again."

Otter left as well and the remaining four of us went into the house. Adam broke the silence, "That has to be the weirdest experience I have had. Is it my imagination or does that guy look and act just like Ralph?"

The rest of us nodded and Alex proceeded to tell the story of that morning's experience at the Muffin Break.

"He can be our back up drummer," Alex said as he ended the story. That took us all by surprise. Immediately all faces turned towards me to see my reaction.

"It makes sense," I said. "He is the closest player to me or Ralph that we have come across. If something happens to me or my ability to play is hampered then he would be the logical choice. Otter doesn't like him, but like you said, he is a backup. I don't plan on being replaced anytime soon."

Adam grinned like a nasty little boy when he said, "Good idea to have a back up. Let's face it, you're always getting into trouble." We all laughed as what he said was so true.

"But we really don't know anything about him, do we?" Danny asked. "What if the guy turns out to be a freak or a druggie or worse? You two just met him today. I think you should hold off on anything definitive until you have gotten to know him better."

"You're Right Dan," Alex said, "For now we will keep our intentions to ourselves and see what comes of our interactions with him. I have to agree with Mo and Otter, it seems odd this guy showing up now. I can't help feeling like there is more to this story." All was quiet for a moment, all lost in our own thoughts about Tim.

After that day, teaching Tim became an all-consuming passion for me. He attended all our gigs. It was like a crash course. I even had him come up and play a few songs at some of the smaller gigs we played so he could get a feel for the bigger experience as he had never played anywhere but in a garage. When he played I would stand in the crowd and watch him. It was so much like watching Ralph. We took turns telling him stories about Ralph and how much he reminded all of us of him. Alex and I also worked on him about going back to school. We agreed this year would be over in a few weeks so there was no point in starting until the fall.

With school ending and summer approaching, Danny and my love, Adam, were getting excited about their summer adventure. Maybe while they traveled through Europe together they'd even make some art contacts for down the road. He and Danny would go off and hammer out details while I was either rehearsing or studying.

On weekends and afternoons I spent every extra minute I had with Adam, running through the woods and taking pictures with him. Then I got to spend lots of time alone in his apartment while he and Danny were off making plans. But then he'd come home and we'd have our precious nights together. Classes started to wind down and school became more about getting ready for exams.

With so much time at his place, I started leaving more of my things there. One day, after picking me up from school and arriving at his home, he showed me how he had rebuilt his closet to be a walk-in and already half of the space was filled with my stuff.

Adam thought of everything. He never added burden to my thoughts, or my anxieties. Just seemed to know what was best for us, and for me, and went ahead. Building that closet removed the need for me to be home in the evenings on school days as he could easily drive me to school in the mornings.

I couldn't wait for school to end, it had been a rough school year for me, having had so many issues last year. My grades had dropped and it had taken a huge effort to bring them back up. Being consistent had required a big effort what with balancing this new band career, and a boyfriend.

Also, Matt, Pat and Eddy had all graduated last year so this year had been different. My best friend Chrissie was making friends elsewhere so we rarely saw each other. Lots had changed. Pat had moved, Eddy was working in security as a door man while attending the police academy to be a cop. Gig night was really the only time we saw him anymore.

Next year it would be Alex, Otter and me graduating so we could just focus on being famous. Danny and Adam were now done art school and moving into their respective careers. They wanted to open their own gallery when they got home from Europe. Ace still had one more year of university but already offers were coming in for summer internships. Everything was changing so quickly just as Ace had predicted. Maybe this was the real cause of my nightmares? Change. I had always had a hard time with it. Despite loving change it also carried endings and those are what scared me most...

Canada day came and we had a celebration at our house combined with a bon voyage party for the guys. I gave Adam a coiled notebook so he could write his memoirs. Taped inside the back cover was his poem, the one I had read in his car the first time we had met. The one he had written for me. Alex and I bought Danny a camera so he could take lots of photos and share them with us when they returned.

Adam and I left early to spend our last night together at his house, Ace, Danny and Alex were going to come by in the morning and pick us up and we would travel to the airport to say goodbye for eight long weeks. It was late when we arrived at Adam's so I lit the candles and he poured us some wine.

"Are you hungry?" he asked.

"Only for you," I answered with my best seductive smile.

He smiled and pulled me close to him, "Montana what are you going to do all summer without me?"

"Oh I don't know, perhaps I'll find myself a boy toy to keep me occupied," I answered.

"You're something," he laughed. I smiled. Truth is I had asked myself that so many times. It was hard to contemplate life without Adam for a day, never mind 8 weeks.

"Montana, I am telling you -- not requesting -- that you cannot get into any trouble while I'm gone. Please, you've done really well this past year. I don't want to have to fly back and find you've been beaten up or sick, or hospitalized or anything. Promise me you won't get into trouble this summer?"

He was tickling me as he said it and I was laughing but I knew he meant it so I promised to keep myself as safe as possible.

"I have something for you but no laughing Adam, promise?" He promised so I handed him an envelope with a drawing in it that I had been working on forever. Neither Adam nor Danny had proved able to get past my stubborn streak and show me how to draw. I would get frustrated and impatient and quit every time one of them tried.

The truth was that I hated not being naturally good at something. They had to show me how to see in order to show me how to draw and that pissed me off. I just wanted to be able to do it. I know that sounds immature but whatever, it's the truth. The last few months learning to see and draw had become a goal. I now viewed it as a need vs some unwanted duty being thrust upon me. So, Danny helped me with a drawing of Adam sprawled out on his bed.

"No laughing," I repeated as he took the envelope from my hands and opened it. A huge grin spread across his face.

"Now, was that so bad?" he asked teasing, but with a very pleased voice. He spent some time examining it, probably analyzing and seeing things that I had no idea of, perhaps studying my use of line and shadow. You know even if you're not a great artist, you still have a signature style, the way you express and I was pretty sure what Adam was looking at was the emerging style or type of artist I would be, or rather, could be if I ever pursued it.

"Thanks Mo, you did a great job," he spoke sincerely, as he leaned over for a kiss. But I could never help a moment to be a brat so I stuck out my tongue and he kissed that. I laughed and dashed off, and for the rest of the evening we played catch me if you can, and had great fun doing it.

Early the next morning my brothers came and picked us up. With the exception of Danny, this was their first time seeing Adam's colossal mansion. They looked impressed and Ace was obviously uncomfortable. I gave them a tour while Adam and Danny went over their last minute pre-flight checklist. It was funny to see Ace as speechless as I had been the first time I saw the Northrop estate.

We piled in Ace's car. Although not the nicest, it was still the biggest with lots of room in the trunk for the guys' backpacks. My mind was occupied during the drive with images of the last time we drove Danny to the airport for his New York trip. I couldn't bear to lose him so I practically had to be dragged away from him.

I had been running on empty back then, keeping my feelings to myself. Those feelings finally exploded leaving me injured after being jumped by Mercy and her damn gang of losers. I had needed to feel alive, but life kept me feeling trapped and angry. I hadn't realized until the airport that time how much I needed my older brother there for me.

When it was time for them to board we said our final goodbyes, this time I didn't go running after Danny or Adam, I mentally pulled up my big girl panties and walked out of the airport with Ace and Alex. Once we were in the car I said, "Hey big brother looks like we are back to the three of us, wonder what type of mischief Alex and I can get into this time?"

I winked at Alex as I said it.

"Damn Montana they've been gone five minutes and already your trying to give me gray hair. What's your problem, can't you think positive for crying out loud?"

Alex and I erupted in laughter, "That was easy," I finally choked out. "Ace I'm just pulling your leg, I mean really, would I announce my plans to give you gray hair? No way, I would just go ahead and do it."

He grinned as shook his head he said, "You guys will be seventeen in a few months, I'm feeling old."

"Old, my gosh you sound like dad, he started griping about age when he was thirty. Old men don't wear caps!" I said as I grasped his and sat on it.

"Montana, give it back."

"No, I answered teasingly and passed it to Alex.

"Give it back now, or I won't be responsible for what I do when we park," he said. His eyes went dark, not dangerously so, but dark enough to let us know Alex and I would have our hands full in a Stanford sibling wrestling match.

"No way," I said, grinning with delight as Alex tossed the hat back to me. Ace was laughing when he parked the car. Alex and I jumped out and made for the front door. Just as we were attempting to get inside, Ace grabbed me so I threw the hat to Alex.

Where I am fast, Alex is lightning quick. He ran to the backyard with Ace just behind him. I followed and a game of pig in the middle began with us laughing so hard we all eventually collapsed on the grass, tears running, our chests heaving with the effort of fending off our giant of a brother. "You two are terrible," he gasped out. We laughed at him. Eventually we peeled ourselves off the ground and went inside. Things were pretty quiet around our house after that and for the first week or two I stuck pretty close to home.

Alex, Otter and I hung out all the time. When we needed a break from rehearsal we would head down to 7 11 for a drink and then go to second beach for a swim and to hang with our buddies. Those were great days, just hanging, jamming and swimming.

Otter got a girlfriend that summer, Emma the girl from the Muffin Break. He was pretty stoked about having her. She was a real sweetheart. It was nice to see him so happy and excited for a change. Otter had not had any serious relationships and as yet had never really held the spotlight. With the band it was usually Alex, the rest of the time it was usually me. It was nice to see him have some glory and be the talk of the group for a bit.

We had some major gigs coming up and I wanted to help Tim out so I gave him half of my gigs in the more questionable venues. I know that pleased Ace. Tim got the full payment for the gigs he played which still left enough money for me

from mine. Plus, I still got the 10% booking fee.
Alex was writing more and some really good stuff.
Otter even threw in a song every once in a while
and even though they wouldn't make us famous
they were good enough to play at our gigs. We had
a gig in *Kitsilano*, a neighborhood across the bay on
the west side where my first gig had been after
Ralph had left the band. Eddy set up and stayed to
keep an eye on me. Alex and I saw many of our old
west side buddies there. Tim, who had come along,
got quite a few looks from kids who had known
Ralph.

Leigh, Ralph's old girlfriend came over to
introduce herself to Tim and I could see she was
still the same person and still up to her old games.
So, I felt I did Tim a favour when I got rid of her
with a well-timed, "Get lost." The truth was that it
was a bit of revenge on my part. Last time I had
seen Leigh was when Ralph and I were still dating
and she was sitting on his lap making out.

It had been a month since the guys had left and I was thrilled to be functioning so well without them. There had been no issues and everything was feeling easy, effortless. I was enjoying sharing the spotlight with Tim. Somehow it made me feel like I was giving back.

Ralph had taught me and asked nothing of me but that I show up. Now I was teaching Tim and asking nothing of him but to show up. Still, the nightmares continued and they seemed to be more frequent. Alex would sometimes give me questioning looks in the morning but I declined to share. I didn't fully understand them and I didn't feel like sharing them with anyone would help me.

In the material world all was good, but in the deepest part of the night, something was haunting me and robbing me of the peace I so desired....

I was relaxed and fully into our playing as our second set wound down. I now believed that Ace's premonition was unfounded, but then a tall decent looking guy came up to me and asked me if I wanted to smoke a joint. I said no and walked off to join Otter back stage. Mr. Good Looking continued to hang around close to the stage. Otter and Tim noticed him and asked if I knew him. I said no, but told them he had invited me outside to smoke a joint. They asked if I wanted them to get rid of the spook. I said no, I'm being Ms. Independent and besides, the last thing I needed was a big deal to be made out of what could be nothing....

We went into our third set, me feeling a little less free spirited than I had in the previous two sets. After the third set I didn't see Mr. Tall and Creepy and was beginning to think I was suffering from a simple case of paranoia when he just appeared out of nowhere as I checked my gear. "Hi," he said. "Hi back," I muttered, not really looking at him but looking through my lashes to see where the guys were...Alex was talking to the club manager. Eddy was at the door, Tim and Otter were nowhere in sight. Damn, I thought. As I was straightening up to excuse myself, T and C suddenly grabbed my arm and I let out a startled yelp as I felt a prick in my skin. Then he was gone, and I was left with a shiny needle sticking out of my forearm. Alex turned around, as usual, picking up on my instant distress. He grabbed the needle and removed it.

I was horrified. I knew it must be a drug, hopefully not a deadly one, but still a drug! Alex reached me just as I hit the floor and then, nothing. When I awoke Alex was sitting by the bed looking none too shabby. That's good, I thought. That meant I hadn't been out long. Sensing more than hearing, Alex turned and looked at me. "Heroin," he said before I could ask.

"Ace is on his way. You haven't been out long, a half hour maybe, and we got you into Eddy's car and here in record time. So, the heroin hadn't been in your system very long. They detoxed you immediately…Dr. Treakle just happened to be here tonight, so we lucked out."

Alex had to call Ace as both he and I were underage and they wouldn't accept Eddy as a replacement for a family guardian. Tim had been trying to explain to the doctor in emergency what had happened when Dr. Treakle walked by. He recognized Alex and came over to see what the fuss was about. Dr.Treakle took over, and had me detoxed and in recovery within 15 minutes.

Ace showed up. Then, with a list in hand of possible ill effects we left the hospital and headed for home. I flopped on the couch when we got there and Ace brought me a cold cloth for my warm head and a blanket for my shivering body. I felt like I was severely drunk and had a hangover at the same time

"Are you okay?" Ace asked, as he eased himself onto the side of the couch where I was lying down. I nodded and took the glass of water that Alex handed me. He didn't say a word so but I could see the expectation in his body. I knew what he wanted. For me to quit the band, to be the bigger person.

Alex sat across from us not saying a word. He and I shared everything. He knew what Ace wanted to hear. Alex sighed almost imperceptibly. Ace certainly didn't notice, however that slight movement of his indicated to me that he would accept whatever the outcome.

I sighed in an obvious manner, indicating I was ready to broach the subject of the band. What I really wanted was to tell Ace to screw off. *Shit happens, so leave me alone to continue my journey.*

"What do you want from me Ace?"

He looked as if he was going to make a snarky remark but he took a breath instead and said, "You know Montana, I am looking for you to say that you are ready to take responsibility for what happened. And even though it was not your fault in the least… leave the band." I had a million thoughts flit through my brain and almost as many comebacks…. The truth was, I was tired of fighting with him, of fighting to do what I wanted. One thought dominated the rest. You win.

"Okay," was all I said.

"Okay?"

"Yes. This is me taking responsibility for what I agreed to," I answered as I rose shakily to my feet. "Goodnight," I said, and closed the door to my room.

Red eyes. No messages, but images, ravaged young women. As always, a dead me among them, my empty eyes staring back at me. I floated freely over the bodies. I reached down to close my dead eyes. My dead hand grabbed my arm. In shock I gazed from the arm to the face that held me in a death grip. It was no longer me. It was a face I did not recognize. The man that stared back I did not know but I knew he meant me harm. I tried to pull away as Red eyes laughed in the background. The more I tried to break free the stronger the grip became. And finally, he pulled out a knife. I screamed as the knife came towards me and-- Instantly I was awake.

Alex stood at the end of my bed, he did not reach out to comfort me but asked, "Who is Mr. Red Eyes?" Then he turned around and went back to bed. He was sleep walking. He hadn't done that in years but had done it often enough when we were kids.

I got out of bed and choked down a glass of whiskey. I wanted to talk to Adam badly to let him know what had happened. It would be morning now so I gave his hotel a ring. He and Dan had already checked out. I went down the list and the dates of where they would be and phoned the hotel he would be arriving at later that day and left him a message.

I tried to sound cool, nonchalant so he wouldn't think anything was wrong. I just said I missed him and wanted to hear his voice.

Chapter 3

I had gone back to bed and when I woke up in the morning I had the worst hangover ever. I was muttering as I looked around the kitchen for bloody Mary ingredients. Finally, finding what I needed, I sat down and enjoyed my morning after cure…Nothing else worked liked a bloody Mary. Otter and Tim came for a quick rehearsal. I'd been questioning why we did rehearsals anymore. Really, we were flawless, so unless we were rehearsing new stuff, what was the point? But I guess that wasn't going to be my problem anymore, it would be Tim's.

"Hey guys, I need to talk to you before we start. I have been told I need to take responsibility for last night." (Like it was my fault? Being a girl is so much fun…*NOT!)* "…So I guess Tim will be my replacement." Alex nodded. He knew this was coming. Otter shook his head angrily. He wasn't happy about it and Tim didn't say anything. I began to cry. So, I left the garage as there was nothing else to say. I went for a walk along the seawall. I needed time to be alone to think and sort through all of my feelings. It always seemed that everyone got to do what they loved, what they were passionate about, except me. I was always having to give something up. My life was filled with endings, maybe that was my destiny, always having to say *goodbye*.

On my way, back towards home I wondered what was next for me. I had four more weeks of no Adam or Danny. I would call and tell them of course, and then what…? That song from the Wizard of Oz came to mind…. I could while away the hours, conferrin' with the flowers…. That made me grin, I loved that cowardly lion. I know, I know, the scarecrow sang those lyrics.... If I only had a brain... I'd think about love and art.

Ace and Alex were in the kitchen eating dinner when I arrived. I grabbed some food and joined them at the table. "How are you feeling about your decision?" Ace asked. "Alex told me about your speech to the band this morning. It must have been hard for you".

"Endings Ace. My life just gets going and then something ends. I am confused as to why this is my lot in life and why I am not simply able to pursue my dreams like everyone else." No one spoke after that and dinner was a silent affair with each to their own thoughts. I cleared the dishes and washed and went to bed. I lay there feeling lethargic but antsy. I couldn't sleep and I knew why. That drug from last night was playing with me. I got up and got dressed. Dan had installed alarms on the windows after a Halloween party a few years back. I disarmed them (of course!), and snuck out my window and headed to the 7-11 to get some coke for my rum. Seems Tim had the same idea and we stopped to chat for a moment.

"Hey" I said.

"Hey yourself," he returned the greeting.

"What are you doing down here?" I asked.

"Just hanging. I couldn't sleep, and you?"

"Same."

"Are you feeling the effects of the drugs still?"

"I think so," I sighed.

"Do you want to take a walk?"

"Sure," I answered.

We walked, drank and talked and we asked each other lots of questions. Mostly about our pasts. He told me he had tried heroin once. It was a bad ride he said, and he could just imagine what I must be experiencing.

"Montana I feel really bad about this whole thing, you are the rightful drummer, not me."

"Hey Tim, don't worry about it. My time has come to an end, at least for the moment. Just as Ralph's did," I added with a catch in my voice.

"Is that what this whole thing is about, your reason for giving in so easily…Ralph? 'Cause I'm not him and this should not be because of what you think he would want."

I didn't say anything. Could he be right? I pondered. I had not considered that guilt may be playing its part in this. No. I had agreed to Ace's strong suggestion and that was all. But I couldn't help thinking that somehow destiny was also playing a part.

I changed the subject and we continued to drink and walk until almost dawn. I finally felt able to sleep. Tim walked me home and I waved just before sliding in through my window. I put on my pajamas and went out to the kitchen to get some juice.

Ace was working inventory that day and was up early.

"You're up early," he said. I grunted and got my juice and headed off to bed. I fell asleep immediately and had a restless sleep, filled with bizarre dreams. I remember reading once that in some cultures it is believed that we create our universe while we sleep. Every time I had weird dreams I wondered what I was creating.

"Montana, are you awake? It's time for dinner." I shuffled into the kitchen in my pajamas and sat down at the table. "Nice to see you finally decided to wake up," Alex said. I just grunted and started eating. Ace was back home and now realized I'd been sleeping all day.

"Montana do you want to talk about anything, like how your feeling? Open up about the band thing, what your plans are, anything?"

"No."

"Don't travel that path again Montana, please, you know what happens and it's nothing good."

"Going back to bed." I left and I knew I was acting like a three year old, totally self-absorbed, but I didn't care. Ace was right of course and I did recognize this path. I had traveled it many times before and always when I was running from something. Despite knowing this, I felt powerless to stop it, unable to control myself. I felt unable to control my world. I was having a momentary lack of direction, add a dose of adversity and Voila! You have the ingredients for a full scale retreat. I snuck out my window, but not without making up a fake person and placing it in my bed in case Ace checked in on me.

I was restless, moody and anxious as I headed to 7-11. I was almost to the door when I spotted Tall and Creepy from the other night. He was talking to Mercy…MERCY? The light bulb flickered on and I was seeing what was happening. My worst enemy had sabotaged me again. Why was I not surprised?

I wished I had Eddy with me right then, he would have gone ballistic all over Mr. Creepy and Mercy. Then my eyes widened in surprise as Tim showed up and joined in the conversation with them. I couldn't believe it. He was conversing with my worst enemy and he knew it. I had told him about Mercy and the things she had done. He was shaking his head and finally, walked away angry. I didn't hear what they said but the message seemed pretty clear. I went home-- minus one rum and coke-- to think about what I had just witnessed. As I crawled through my bedroom window my light suddenly came on, Ace was standing there. "That was pretty fast, did you forget something?"

I was caught red handed and I wanted to tell him about what I just saw, but he just said I was grounded and not to bother trying to explain. The next morning I woke early to the sounds of Ace leaving for an early shift. I waited until I heard the last rumblings of his car and then left the house. Despite being grounded I had to find Tim. I needed to know what was going on and Tim clearly had the answers. I found him at the Muffin Break, working. "I need to talk to you," He nodded his head and we went outside. I studied his face for remorse or any other emotion that may betray him but he was a blank slate.

"Tim you know how I feel about Mercy, right? I mean I explained to you what she has done and how she has treated us right from the moment we all met her. I have shared her evil and vile plots." He nodded. "Then you of all people should understand my confusion when I saw the two of you together last night and you clearly knew each other. What the hell is going on?" Now his face betrayed some emotion, conflict and maybe regret…. "You and Mercy were with that tall creep who shot me up with heroin, that tells me you knew who he was the night I was stuck. You knew that she sent him and you never told me. How could you?"

I was starting to get upset. I was so sick of betrayal, why couldn't people just be who they appeared to be? On the inside I was feeling distraught, on the outside I was my cool West End self and I stared him down with my blue eyes glittering dangerously. "I haven't told anyone yet, but I will, and whether you live or not will depend on if you tell me the truth here and now." He looked thoughtful, clearly weighing out what was worse, Mercy or my brothers. My brothers won. Tim took his lunch break and spilled the beans.

"I knew Mercy from school in Abbotsford, she and I even dated for a very brief time, which is when I tried the heroin. Mercy's mom and my mom are friends, they are both single moms and they used to go out once in a while for drinks." He continued. "When they moved downtown Carol, Mercy's mom, suggested that we move down here too and we finally did. Mercy and I reconnected and she mentioned she had an enemy named Montana who had done some nasty stuff to her and she was plotting out some revenge. She said now was a good time to strike as your protection was away on holidays and your best buddy Eddy was now working so he wasn't watching your back like he used to."

"Tall and Creepy and the doorman you told me about are friends with Nick, they all hang together. Mercy had worked out a deal with Nick to have those two guys do that to you. I didn't know until our walk the other night, the real story around you and Mercy. So I went to the 7-11 last night to tell her I wasn't helping them anymore. That they were on their own."

"How did you help them?" I wanted to hear every detail.

"The other half of the plan was to destroy you as a drummer so you wouldn't play anymore. I would replace you and with you out of the way, Mercy would be the belle of the ball once again. Mercy saw that I was a dead ringer for Ralph and knowing your feelings for him she saw a way to play on your heart strings. At the same time she hit you with enough issues that finally Ace would step in and make you quit playing. She nailed it because that is exactly what has happened, and I am sorry for it."

This was a huge scheme; the implications were overwhelming. I didn't know how to react. Mercy must really, really hate me, like only evil hates good. "Well it worked out for you didn't it? Alex and I welcomed you in like a lost brother." I sounded cold and distant.

"No. See, that is the thing Montana. The first time I played with you guys I knew you had something special, that you should be the drummer, not me. I will tell the guys that this is all a mistake, I should have already but to be honest I was really enjoying hanging out with you, and I knew that would end the moment you knew the truth." I didn't respond to him, what could I say? The deception just to bring me down was overwhelming, way too much for me to absorb.

"Tim I don't know how I feel about this, or you. There is a lot to think about. I need some time alone." I walked home and when I got there Alex was in the kitchen.

"Ace just phoned for you, I told him you were sleeping, what's going on?"

Alex always knew when something was up, and I wanted to tell him so badly. But he had to play that night and the timing was all wrong, he needed to stay focused.

"We'll talk later," I answered cryptically. "I have a phone call to make. I dug out the phone number that I had for where Danny and Adam were staying in Italy. A familiar voice answered the phone but it was not the one I expected, in fact it was the last one I wanted to hear. "heeio,who's zees?"

"Katya, its Montana, I need to speak with my brother." She didn't say anything for a minute,

"Katya I really need to talk to Danny is he there?" She said he wasn't and then hung up the phone. Ugh, I couldn't stand that woman. She had stayed with us just before Ralph had been killed and she spent her entire time seducing everyone she came across.

Let's face it. She was gorgeous, very beautiful, perfect in fact, but she was mean. Not evil like Mercy, just mean spirited. Well, what would you expect? She was the only daughter of a very wealthy family, part of Parisian aristocracy.

What was she doing in Italy and what was she doing in Adam and Danny's hotel room? A part of me registered that I needed to have a discussion at a later time with my boyfriend, if he still was my boyfriend. But for now I needed a plan and as I had nobody but me on my side I was going to have to act alone and quickly. I needed the element of surprise.

Hours went by, Alex was getting ready to leave and Ace had not arrived home yet. I thought it was worth trying to get Ace to listen to me, "Hey Alex, when is Ace supposed to be getting home?"

"He has a date with Kristine tonight, so late," he said.

"Is he coming to the gig?"

"No, he said being as you're not going to be there, then he didn't need to be there." Figures I thought, he always made me feel like I was interrupting his life.

"I'm coming with you guys." A plan was forming in my mind. I knew she would be there and I wasn't going to miss the opportunity to confront her.. I would think on my feet once I saw who else was with her.

"Do you really think that is a good idea?" Alex asked.

"Yes, and I think you will too when you see who else shows up tonight."

He shrugged and said, "Whatever," and we left.

I sat in the farthest corner from the stage so I could see who entered the club and keep my eye on the band as well. Tim glanced in my direction but we did not greet each other. I was dressed discreetly in black leather and had a cap on with my hair tucked up, and the place was dark. I felt certain I could survey the comings and goings without being noticed.

The band was into song three when Mercy, Nick, the doorman from the other club and Mr. Tall and

Creepy and some other scumbag not worth the air they sucked walked in. They walked right up to the front. When they sat down Mercy waved to Tim. He just glared at her and she laughed. Alex and Otter glanced at Tim and then Mercy. Discreetly Alex looked to where I hid in the corner. He got it. I knew he knew I had been betrayed. Otter had been right from the beginning in thinking something was not right with Tim and how he had just suddenly appeared in our lives.

Watching them put me in a rage . The more I watched her revel in my apparent absence, the clearer I got on what I was going to do. I had to call her out. I had not fought since I had been jumped almost two years earlier and then it had been by Mercy and her posse. The irony that here we were again but she didn't know it yet was not lost on me. Nor was the promise to avoid trouble that I had made Adam. But this was different. I was fighting for me, for my right to play, for my dream. I would never let her take that away from me.

As I watched Mercy's group, assessing the strengths and the weaknesses, my nightmare was complete when Mercy's remaining three crew members walked in. I sat farther back in my seat. It would not help me if they saw me before I wanted them to. If I called out Mercy now, it would be eight against one.

I needed to think... how could it be a fair fight?

Three songs later, the first set was done and the band had a break. I snuck behind the stage to talk to Alex. He was just drinking some water when I walked backstage to talk to him.

"What the hell is going on? You *knew* they were going to be here, and that is why you wanted to be here tonight?"

"Yes, yes and yes Alex. I have to call her out."

"Are you insane? Don't you remember what happened last time?"

"Listen Alex, I have a plan. For this to be a fair fight her posse can't know that I 'm here. I want you to go out there and tell her you want to talk to her privately and bring her out the back door to the alley."

"Why Montana, why are you doing this?"

"Ask him," I said, pointing to Tim as he walked backstage and saw Alex and me talking.

Tim froze, "I told you Mo, it is just like I said. She will lord that she won over your territory and systematically destroy everything you have worked for."

"Like hell she will," Alex said. "Tim, what is going on? Did you know about this?"

Tim nodded his head and was about to explain but we were running out of time. "Listen, you guys have to go back up in a few. At the end of the next set do as I ask Alex and meet me in the back alley, okay?"

Alex nodded and I heard him say, "Tim, If something happens to my sister you will pay for it." Then they were back on stage and too far away for me to hear anything more of their conversation. At the end of the second set I made my way to the alley. I stood in a doorway across from the back door of the club and waited. Seconds later, Alex and Mercy came out. She was giggling and hanging on his arm looking like the cat that got the bowl of cream. She always did have a thing for Alex. I stepped out of a doorway.

"Hello Mercy, I see you're still up to your little tricks." She blanched for a moment but recovered in lightning speed.

"Tonight it ends. I am calling you out, hand to hand, one on one. If you win, Tim stays and you can go to any gig, wherever, whenever. If I win, you and your posse leave us alone forever and never come to a gig ever, and I mean ever again, do you agree?"

She didn't like it, but our West End code didn't allow her to turn me down, so she agreed. We circled each other. In my peripheral vision I could see Tim and Alex watching us. Then Otter opened the door to join them so I was momentarily distracted and that's when she lunged.

She was wearing a pair of metal knuckles. She must have been hiding them in her pocket. It was . good that I'm fast and know how to duck. I threw a return punch and made contact with her right eye, she staggered back a few feet and then came at me again.

This time she caught me in the ribs with her brass knuckles. She grinned and I grimaced as we both heard the crack. I nailed her back this time, twice. Once in the head and once in the stomach and she went down. I jumped on top of her and gave her a few more punches to finish her off.

I got off her, "I won, you lost. Now get out of here." I turned to make my way back to the club. She lay on the ground sputtering blood. I heard her

moving and was turning towards her as Alex yelled,
"Watch out!" I felt something cold and hard go into
my back. I went down on my knees and felt my
back; a knife blade was sticking out.

"Otter, quick. Run and call an ambulance now."
"Tim, don't let her get away, she's going down for
this. Otter, call the cops." Alex was barking out
orders while holding me. Someone must have seen
the fight and told everyone in the club. Patrons
poured out the back to see what had happened, and
when Nick and the others saw me with a knife in
my back they took off, leaving Mercy behind.

I was feeling faint as the distant sounds of sirens
filled the night, Alex held me, and for a few
moments it was just he and I. He was sending
healing vibes into me and talking to me in low
tones. "Good thing you were wearing leather and
her knife wasn't really big. I think she missed the
major organs, but I have to pull it out Montana. So
brace yourself."

I felt pressure and then agony, and then nothing. The last thing I heard before I passed out was my scream and the pitched wailing of the ambulance. I woke up some time later and my first conscious thought was, I should have known, damn Mercy and her dirty fighting. She was beneath any code. My next thought was I can't feel anything , I must be on good drugs. The room looked familiar, I was sure I had been in this one before. I looked to the chair beside me and saw that Ace was occupying it. He had his eyes closed but I could tell he wasn't sleeping. He must have sensed me staring at him, because he opened his eyes.

"Hey chief."

"Hey peanut, are you trying to make me old? I would thrash you if you weren't so helpless," he said with a smile.

"Did Alex tell you the whole story?" I asked

"Mostly, but he has been with the police most of the time. Tim and Otter also, giving background info as this was attempted murder. Mercy outdid herself this time and we are pressing charges."

I contemplated that for a minute before saying, "Ace, is that the right thing to do? You know we wouldn't usually do something like that. We let people off with conditions."

He shook his head, "Not this time Peanut. This is not a few broken ribs or some stitches. Do you understand what happened tonight? You were stabbed. She just missed your kidney and spleen. If she had hit them we would not be having this conversation right now, you would be dead."

A silent tear escaped down his face, "I should kill you and Alex myself for getting yourselves into this."

"Don't blame Alex, Ace. He didn't know why I was tagging along tonight, he told me to stay home but I went anyway. It is my entire fault, as usual. I waited to talk to you but Alex said you were on a date and wouldn't be home until late. I tried talking to Danny but Katya wouldn't tell him I was on the phone."

"Wait a minute; slow down, what are you talking about?"

So I went back to the beginning and told him what I saw at 7-11 and then my conversation with Tim and how I called Danny and Katya had answered the phone and what she had said. How I had waited for him to come home and then finally making my own decision.

"You know Ace it would have been fine if she hadn't fought dirty, she had brass knuckles on too."

"That would explain the cracked ribs you have, again, I need to go and make a call, and I'll be right back."

A moment later in walked Tim, "do you mind if I come in?"

I waved him in.

"Montana, I'm really sorry about everything that has happened. I had no idea all that was going to go down and I didn't know Mercy had become so nasty. I'm still in shock."

Ace came back in took one look at Tim and said, "Out." I gave him an apologetic smile and out he went.

"How can you talk to him after what he did?"

"He is just a pawn Ace, just like those other two guys who stuck me with the needle, and attacked me in the bathroom, just pawns in her nasty game. It's not their fault--"I could see Ace was about to explode so I hurried on, "--and those other two can rot for all I care, but Tim-- he knew less and didn't want to participate in the first place. Just give him a break.... So what is the scoop, how long do I have to stay?"

"I should leave you here alone for two weeks. That would teach you a lesson." he said with a grin.

"I can't feel anything below my rib cage, what type of drugs do they have me on?"

"I don't know," he frowned, "let me go and talk to the doc." Once again I was alone, lying there waiting. Given how everything had turned out I couldn't help thinking back to when I first met Mercy. She seemed so together. Sure, we challenged each other, but I thought we could have been friends...at first. We were both great looking girls with an attitude. I could remember some of the conversation we had after we downed all that alcohol on the beach and smoked that joint. I thought she understood. About me, about my brothers. The West End. The code. It seemed to really click with her, but instead of seeing me as an ally, I was just competition. She couldn't even have an honour fight without cheating. I guess the fact I could see through her act and call her on all that insecurity...she just couldn't stand to be seen.

The phone rang. Everyone who knew me was here so I wasn't going to answer it at first but it wouldn't stop ringing so I picked it up.

"Montana."

"Danny. How did you know where I was?"

"Ace called, are you okay? I'm really sorry about Katya. I was here when you called and I still can't believe she hung up on you."

"It's okay Danny, I made a choice and did what I needed to do."

"Apparently," Danny said dryly. "Adam wants to talk to you." I winced. He was the only one I had made a promise to for the summer and I let him down.

"Montana, I've been worried sick, are you okay? Tell me what happened." So again, I told the story in the most abbreviated version possible as I was getting tired. I was yawning by the time I had finished.

"We are flying home tomorrow, I will see you soon."

"Don't worry about me," I yawned again, "I'll be fine, just enjoy yourself and I'll see you in a few weeks. Wait, Ace is back and he wants to talk to you."

"Montana, the doctor is just wheeling you down for an x-ray I'll see you in a few minutes." I nodded, too tired by now to speak.

"Hey Adam, did Mo tell you everything? Listen, there is more that she doesn't know about yet. The knife missed her organs but the tip pierced the side of her spine. She can't feel anything from the bottom of her ribs and down."

Silence came from the other end of the phone, "Adam, did you hear me? Montana may be paralyzed."

Adam sighed, "Tell me the bottom line Ace."

"They are taking x-rays now but the consensus so far is it is paralysis, and hopefully temporary. For how long no one is sure, possibly as long as six months. It will depend on the therapy. The staff has a good reputation but there is a huge waiting list. She waits her turn just like everyone else."

There was a pause on the other end of the phone; "All right Ace, I'll pass this along to Dan and we will see you in a day or two." Adam tried to hang up the phone but he missed the cradle so Ace heard him go off.

"Damn! Why, why is she so impulsive? And why did I think nothing would happen while I was gone!" Normally so controlled, Adam could be heard stomping around, seemingly running into furniture. It sounded like a glass broke. "Damn that Mercy! She has *always* been bad news! So much for Belgium... --" Click. Just then, whatever Adam crashed into knocked the phone back into the cradle and the connection was lost.

When I came back in Ace said that Danny and Adam would be back in a day or two. "Oh I told those guys to stay there and have a good time. I'll be just fine in a few days." Alex walked in and sat at the end of my bed. He was looking very tired. I guess the cops had worn him out.

"Does she know yet?" he asked, looking deep into my eyes. A look that I had not seen from him before. He was silently talking to me, telling me to be brave. But still, his look was one of resignation and Ace's was the same. None of it made any sense. I passed out.

When I came to, my brothers' silence and weird looks pissed me right off. I demanded to know what was going on. "Listen you. You tell me what's got you both acting so weird or I swear I will chase you both down and tackle you until you do." Ace waved Alex to wait a minute.

"Look Montana, there is no easy way to say this so I will come right out with it. The knife nipped the edge of your spinal cord and injured some nerves.

The doctors don't know how long it will take for you to be up and around, if ever. They are optimistic, but these things go differently for everyone."

"What are you saying Ace, that I'm paralyzed?"

I started to hyperventilate, which hurt like hell because of the ribs. I started to tremble. Alex grabbed my hand and squeezed tight. "Montana, it's going to be alright. This is not how your story ends. Mo, please, you're going to be okay."

I lost it, and moments later the staff entered and gave me something to knock me out. When I woke next both Ace and Alex were still there. "Hey," I said. "I guess I won't be climbing out my bedroom window anytime soon."

Despite the gravity of the situation, Ace began to laugh, Alex joined in and the doc found us a few moments later laughing so hard we had tears. For a moment the doc looked completely taken back, and then smiled at our merriment.

"Will I ever walk again," I asked the doc?
Please, please, please say yes. Please say yes.

"Actually, the damage is quite minor so we are optimistic that you will have a full recovery. We just don't know how long it will take. Could be as little as a few months or up to a year. A lot of how your recovery takes is up to you. The more aggressive you are with your therapy and positive with your thinking the better progress you will make."

I looked to Alex, he felt my turmoil, he always did, and he looked exhausted poor boy. He would have felt the trauma and pain of course. He always did. But there was no therapy being offered for that. Somehow along the way of growing he had learned to deal with it and let it go, unlike me.

The good doctor continued, "The hospital will give you as many physiotherapy appointments as we can to help with the process...."

Ace interjected, "Our brother and Montana's boyfriend are on their way home from Europe. We will all share in the responsibility of bringing her here as often as necessary."

Dr. Kelso smiled and left the room. "Ace, Adam can't see me like this. Please phone him back. I don't want him to see me helpless, useless, stupid...." The events rolled through my mind and my mind was rejecting everything. I suddenly couldn't handle the enormity of the situation. I began to sob,

"Please leave me alone. Go away."

"Montana, I'm not leaving you and you are not retreating into yourself this time. I won't let you. Now stay with me you hear? Stay with me. Look at me now. You are still you: Young, beautiful, vibrant. This is just a little set back, and we can get through this, okay? There is nothing we can't get through if we just stick together. Don't disappear."

I looked at Alex; he was holding my hand. I could feel him willing Ace's words into my being, his life force spreading through me like a warm blanket. "Okay chief, I can do that. When do we start?" I said, squeezing Alex's hand.

"That's my girl, tough as nails all the way." And he gave my other hand a squeeze as hugs would hurt my broken ribs. I stayed in the hospital that night and went home the next day. My therapy would begin after a few days of rest. I had to take it easy because of the stitches and the cracked ribs.

Before I left the hospital, they changed my bandages and wrapped me back up. We went home and I anxiously awaited the expected arrival of Danny and Adam. Ace made me up a spot on the couch for the night so I could visit with any of our friends that may pop in. Eddy, Pat and Matt were by minutes after we arrived home to see how I was doing.,

"I'm sorry Montana, I should have been there for you," Eddy said.

"Eddy you can't be there all the time, but thanks for thinking you can," I said with a small smile. They left and the three of us were just having some tea, when Adam and Danny burst through the door. They stopped, rooted just inside the front door. Ace stood and went and gave Danny a big hug, and then Adam. Ace's shoulders visibly relaxed at something Adam said and Ace gripped him tighter before letting him go.

Hmm I wondered what that was about. Despite the physical connection with Ace both men had eyes only for me. Probably wondering why I am such an ass and why they love me I thought. How was it possible for Adam to be even better looking than when he left for the trip? He was gorgeous, my Greek god. At least I hoped he was still mine. I wouldn't want to date me. I couldn't imagine why he would.

No one was saying anything and they seemed to resist coming towards me. If they didn't see the disability then it couldn't be real, right? I broke the silence…. "I really missed you guys. It's okay, I'm not broken, well, not completely anyway, right Ace?"

He took his cue, "That's right, we are optimistic for a full recovery."

Danny smiled and came over to give me a little hug. "I've been so worried about you the whole way home," he said.

"I missed you. I feel like a lifetime has passed since you left. I pressed my head into his shoulder and smelled him and smiled, Danny smelled as good as he looked. He'd make someone ridiculously happy one day, I thought.

Danny patted my head and made to get up, "not yet," I whispered, "I'm crying and I don't want anyone else to see."

"You're too funny Mo. No problem. Let me know when you are ready."

"How is Adam?" I whispered.

"Worried sick. Like me, he hasn't slept, he kept trying to get someone at the airport to trade tickets with us. He feels guilty for leaving you, he feels helpless for the condition you're in, and angry. I won't lie, he has had a few ranting spells. You know, just like the rest of us," he smiled and ruffled my hair.

"Montana, give him a smile. He needs you to need him right now." No problem there. I did need him and I wanted him. I took a deep breath and Dan got up and the three of them went to the kitchen to give Adam and me some privacy.

Adam came over and sat down beside me. "I missed you so much Montana. Dan and I saw so many things you would have loved. Next time, you're coming with me so I can keep my eye on you."

"Hold me please," I said. I sighed and sunk as deeply into him as my wrapped ribs would allow. "You feel so good Adam. Mmm... just hold me," I said again. "Stay right here and hold me forever."

After a few minutes he asked if he could survey the damage. There wasn't much to see because of the bandage, but he pulled back the sheet so he could see and actually, you could see blood through the bandage and the bruising around it from the brass knuckles, but nothing else. It was enough to have him wince when he looked at it.

"You promised me you wouldn't get into trouble when I was gone. So as soon as you're healed you're in some big trouble with me," he said in such a manner that I wasn't sure if he was joking or actually had something in mind.

"Well a girl can always hope," I said with my best doe-eyed look, blinking innocently. It was a private joke between the two of us and it had the desired effect of breaking the tension.

"I'm staying here with you Montana."

"What do you mean you're staying here?"

"I'm staying here, by your side until you walk."

"Adam, that is not funny. We don't know how long it could be."

"Two weeks. That is our target, walking in two weeks and I'm going to make sure it happens."

The guys chose that moment to come back to the living room. I looked at Ace. He already knew. Danny piped in; "That's right Montana, Adam's dad has the best in their fields coming to take a look at you and work with you until you're walking."

I was shocked, "Are you insane," I asked Adam, but really I was asking the room. "I can't even guess what amount of money this could cost. No!" I tried to sit up but of course I couldn't. "I can't accept this --we can't accept this. Ace please, tell him this is too much and we can't accept."

Ace looked as if to speak but it was Adam that said; "Montana Stanford this is not charity this is what money is all about, not the country club. Get used to it, because one day what I have will be yours, life, money and all. You will accept my help.

You don't get a choice, and you're going to get better and everything will be great. And I don't want to hear anything else about it."

He slammed his hand down on the coffee table to emphasize that last part. I think we were all in shock except Danny who was grinning. None of us had seen this Adam before. Normally Adam was much more laid back with his opinions and communication of them. He looked to Ace, "Sorry man, but I'm not budging on this one, no disrespect to you."

"None taken," Ace answered with a respectful grin. "It's nice to know that my tyrant of a sister has met her match. Besides, we can't do this on our own. And Montana, your well-being is worth more to me than pride. Sorry, but I would rather see you walking."

Alex tactfully changed the subject and we listened as Danny and Adam told us about Europe. They had been in Paris and had seen the Eiffel tower and gone to the Louvre. England was cold but they had visited some castles and they went to the tower of London and did the pub crawl. They did Wales and Scotland, and were about to leave Italy and head to Germany when they got the call from Ace bringing their trip to a halt. Normally I would have been more interested, I'm sure they saw some cool stuff in all those countries but at that moment I was just irritated with them for quitting their tour.

"I told Ace you guys didn't need to be here. Honestly, it was totally cool with me that you stayed on your tour. I can handle this." They all just stared at me like I had lost my mind. Realizing how dopey what I had said sounded, I turned beet red. The discussion turned to therapy days and times and who would be in attendance those first few days, blah, blah blah...zzzz.

Chapter 4

"Daddy!" There was nothing I could do. He was falling and I was falling behind him, ever farther until not only was he out of reach but finally completely out of sight. Laughter was the soundtrack as Ralph fell past me and again as I reached for him there was nothing I could do. My mother's voice – "No!"

My nightmares got progressively worse leading up to the start of my treatment. The doctors felt I needed a few days to let my wounds knit. Many nights I woke up terrified as receding visions left me shaking. Adam had me propped up in bed. That crazy man was curled up beside me, unmoving until my screaming woke him. He gently shook me awake and shooed my demons away with sweet caresses. I was so weak initially he just let me fall back to sleep.

Falling...falling...hitting the ground. Peeling myself off the concrete and they were back. All the young women. All like me. Red eyes. Seeing them. Helpless to do anything. Torture.

At least three times I awoke to the sounds of my own screaming to find Alex standing at the end of my bed.

He was asleep, unaware that his conscious self was interacting with me. Adam was a little freaked out at first, but once he understood that Alex was sleepwalking and simply tuned into my subconscious emotional channel, he walked him back to his room. In the morning I knew if Alex remembered at all he would think it was just a dream.

The last night before I started therapy, Adam had some questions and I was finally strong enough to answer them. He brought me some water and started in on me. "Mo, what are your terrors about and how long has this been going on?"

"I don't know Adam. A few weeks. I see bodies, I see dead women's bodies all around me and they all have my eyes. It's horrible."

"It's okay, I'm here. Can you forgive me for leaving you so vulnerable?"

"You have nothing to be forgiven for my love. You should be able to travel and go on vacations and not have to worry about death threats on your girlfriend's life. I feel like this crap will never end, will never go away. Like I can't escape my weird destiny."

"It's got to stop. Seems like your visions were prophetic and now they're in reaction to your trauma. How long will it last? Only time will tell, Montana. How did you ever manage for the first while when I was away? Honestly, I expected a call at the end of the first week, so I'm happy you were able to go almost six weeks without me." He grinned as he spoke. He probably really thought that was true.

"Quiet at first. The gigs, the practices, and teaching Tim kept me out of trouble until I got stabbed at the gig with that damn needle. And that is what got Ace's back up and …"

"Wait. What? Back up, what needle?"

"Oh, I thought the guys brought you up to speed on everything. The only reason I found out about Mercy's plot was because I pulled a Mo and went out through the bedroom window and over to 711 late one night." He frowned for a moment but nodded for me to continue.

"Okay, so we had been playing a gig, and a tall, creepy guy had been hanging close all night. When I was checking my equipment before the last set, he stuck me with a needle full of heroin. Alex and Eddy rushed me to the hospital and Dr. Treakle happened to see Alex and asked what was going on. She had my stomach pumped and my body detoxed in no time flat." I could see Adam was dying to say something -- his mouth was open and he looked more like a guppy than usual -- so I rushed on to get the whole story out before he could start.

"Of course Ace did the big, "you made a deal" speech, so I was pretty much forced to hand my sticks over to Tim. Well, as a reaction to the residue of whatever drug was left behind, I couldn't sleep. I wanted to know why it happened. Why me and why drugs? It seemed like such a random act. So, I snuck out. And then I snuck out again. You know, I think this whole paralysis thing was just Ace's way of keeping me grounded! Anyway, it was all planned, Adam. Mercy had a plan to destroy me and she knew you and Dan were gone." I could see Adam processing more information than he had ever wanted to deal with. His brow furrowed as he waited for me to pause.

"Then Katya hung up on me and I had no one to talk to. So I went with Alex to the club. Everything would have been fine if Mercy hadn't been carrying that knife. The brass knuckles I could deal with.

Who knew her hatred ran so deep for me that she would try and kill me?

Adam had been holding his breath and let it out now in a long slow exhalation. "Heroin? She is nothing but evil. I knew it the first time I saw her watching you at the beach. She doesn't hate you for anything you have done Montana, she hates you for what you are; beautiful, talented and loved. She's superficially pretty but she doesn't have any of those other truly valuable things."

"You are very, very lucky to be alive. You know that?" He grabbed my arms squeezing them, gazing intently into my eyes. "You have someone up there watching out for you Montana. I was so worried about you I thought I was going to lose it, and then Danny told me what Katya had done." He stopped squeezing my arms and leaned back on the bed, one arm behind his head, the other sliding under my shoulders.

"What was she doing there anyway?" I asked sullenly. "She's almost as bad as Mercy, you know.

She had it in for me from the first moment she saw me."

"She heard through friends that Danny and I were in Italy and she set up a party for us at our hotel room. I was dealing with the front desk and Danny and Katya went up ahead. That must have been when you called. I told her if you became crippled or died, I would fly back to Europe and no hole was deep enough to hide her from my revenge."

I laughed, "I can picture the haughty indignant look she must have had on her face when you said that. I missed you Adam. I don't want to talk anymore about all this stuff. It doesn't change anything anyway."

"Hmm," he said, "You're still in trouble with me Miss Stanford, and when you're up to snuff, you're going to be very sorry." I grinned but said nothing. A momentary lapse of talking, then he said,

"What do you want to do?"

I grinned, "Are you kidding? You know perfectly well," and I gave him my mischievous grin, " but I will settle for cuddling and kissing, how about that?" We were both exhausted. Kissing only lasted for a few minutes before we passed out.

Early the next morning Danny and Adam had me in the car to go to the hospital. Ace was working and Alex had band practice. Poor Alex, he felt so bad about everything. He blamed himself and the band for my situation. So, he was going to dissolve the band.

I told him it would be the last thing he ever did. Besides, I needed a goal. If he needed me on the drums, then I should get better, right? That was my theory anyway.

There was a team of specialists at the hospital and I was instantly overwhelmed. First, batteries of tests were ordered to re-confirm my condition and to make sure there was nothing else going on. X-rays, ultrasounds, bone scans and other things that I had no idea what they were. I was feeling very disconnected from the experience.

That was to be short-lived however, because two hours later I was in the physiotherapy room and hooked up to a pulsation machine. My ribs were checked and re-wrapped, and then I was ready for the hard stuff. Both Danny and Adam stayed with me at the hospital. They wouldn't leave.

"I told you," Adam said, "I will not leave you during this process, I am here until you are walking."

"Adam, what if I'm not? What if I can't?"

I was wringing my hands together, very near tears. I had a hard time seeing this turning around in two weeks. Neither of them said anything for a minute and then Danny said, "Montana, it is really important that you believe you can and let us worry about the other stuff."

"Okay, but if either one of you feel like spanking me for all the trouble I have caused... now is the time to do it."

They both looked puzzled, "Why?" they asked in unison.

"Because, you silly guys, I can't feel a thing!" They laughed and so did I. In that instant of relief I felt like I could. Releasing the stress seemed to make room for possibility.

Adam came to bed that night and we snuggled until I fell into a deep sleep. The next three days were just a repeat of the first, wrestling me in and out of a wheelchair, then to and from the hospital with Adam in the physiotherapy room watching everything and talking to the doctors to find out what each thing was supposed to do and how it worked, and pushing me with his constant encouragement.

The next night in bed, Adam was running his hands up and down my back and I knew when he rested one on my butt, because although it was a faint sensation it was there. "Adam, is your hand on my butt?"

"Yeah, why?"

"Because I can feel it."

That took a minute to register and then he sat up, "You're kidding, you can feel that?"

"Faintly," I answered.

He was so excited he started rubbing me all over and asking about various spots, but he was going too fast. I asked him to slow down as it was taking time for my brain to register sensation, he slowed down and put his hand on my other hip, "What about here?" he asked.

This was the side my knife wound was on and I tried but I couldn't feel anything and then he ran his hands over my legs and touched my ankles, "Wait," I said, "touch the left one again." There it was again. A spidery sensation, more than ghost feelings. No ability to consciously move anything yet, but a victory, no matter how small.

He got out of bed to go and tell the guys. It made me smile, even as I wept briefly in frustration. He lingered in the doorway. I made him promise not to tell anyone else until I was ready. "Mo, you're a puzzle. This is so exciting, but okay. We can wait a little longer and see what happens."

On day five they had me in a chair by two parallel bars. The idea was to pull myself up and try and shuffle to the other end, where Adam just happened to be standing. As much as I wanted to get to him the problem was the ribs were still healing. Heaving myself up was so painful I was in tears the entire time. Then I was pissed off and in more tears because he got to see me so weak.

I yelled at Adam with more and more frequency. "I can't do this. It's too hard. I just want to be left alone!" Alex was there with us. I didn't care how he saw me. He saw the true me all the time anyway. You can't hide from your twin. But being this angry and feeling this trapped, I lashed out and Adam took the brunt of it that day.

When we got back home that night Ace asked how it went. Alex rolled his eyes and made a fast exit. Adam told him about my outburst and frustration. Ace knew what to do. He always knew what to do when I was like that. He picked me up and sat me on his lap and said, "Okay peanut, just spill," and I ranted and raved all over again, crying all the while until I collapsed in emotional exhaustion.

He just held me while I ranted more and then, when I had calmed down, told me stories about all of us when we were small until he had me laughing and everything was okay. Adam witnessed this little episode and didn't say a word. Later, Ace told Adam that it had taken him years to figure out what to do with me when I totally lost it.

"If you don't let her air her stuff, completely and fully, she retreats inside herself and when she does that, well...you have seen first-hand what happens then. It is very hard to bring her back. Better to keep the lines open and flowing."

We fell asleep early that night. The day had been really intense for us both. I felt bad about how I had treated Adam and it weighed on me as I slipped into sleep. My feelings must have set the tone for my dreams for I woke up screaming, feeling the blade sliding into my back and seeing those red eyes laughing at me.   Adam was waking me, rocking me, soothing me until I fell asleep with his arms wrapped around me. The next day was our sixth and as intense as the previous five. We were packing up for the day when I felt a tingle run up my spine.

"Wait!" I shouted and everyone stopped what they were doing. "I felt a tingle-- there it is again!" I said excitedly. "It's running up and down my spine. Adam, touch my back. Start at the top and run your hands down both sides of my back." He did and I felt it all the way down on both sides right down almost to my thighs, and then lower in my calves and my toes and ankles. I was so excited I would have jumped up and down if I could have.

"Adam you were right, you were right!" This little victory renewed my spirit and gave a nice lift to my belief in myself. When we got back, we burst in and told everyone what had happened. We decided we needed to have a party and so we ordered in pizzas and Ace brought out the beer and I actually got to have some and he didn't say a word.

We had a great time that night. The guys were goofy from the good news and when they got a bit drunk they were really goofy. They ended up having a pillow fight without me. Man, just give me one pillow! But as I reached for one I felt everything for the first time in a week. I stood up—well, I tried. I pushed my way up and stood there swaying for a moment... before I fell back down, but man! What a moment.

Day seven was a huge improvement, I could feel everything, so now we started the hard stuff. Hard for me, it required a lot of effort, and still Adam stayed. He got right in there and kept pushing me on. Every time I got frustrated he would just hug me and tell me I could do it and then we would go again. By the end of day seven, I could move my legs at about 25% of my full mobility. The goal was 100% and I had seven more days to go.

It was all uphill from then on. Every day was like a marathon. Danny stayed with us the last two days to watch the progress. On day fourteen, our last day, the results were in and I was at 90% which was nothing short of a miracle according to the staff at the hospital.

Adam was right, money can be a good thing. The specialists that had been flown in for me for those two weeks cost Adam's dad $250,000. His generous gift had taken at least two months off my recovery time, maybe more. Geoff, Adam's dad, had stopped by at one point to see how his money was being spent.

Adam looked a lot like his dad so I got a picture of what he would look like when he was older, very handsome I thought. I only spent minutes around Geoff, but it was long enough for me to see that the resemblance between the two of them ended there. Personality-wise, they were complete opposites.

Ace and Danny had arranged to take all of us out for dinner along with Adam's parents so we could say thanks properly. On the way home from the hospital that last day, we stopped so I could buy a new outfit. It felt so weird to walk in and out of that store knowing that without Adam I may not have walked at all, ever.

I felt liberated and my spirits were high as we left the store. Adam had picked out the outfit. His sense of style was amazing and with no money restriction he bought what he was drawn to artistically versus the price tag like the rest of us.

I was functionally nowhere near 100% but my body had done a lot in a short window of time, speed healing. The next several weeks, doing what I had been taught would get me the rest of the way physically and energetically. I found moving around exhausting, and just buying one outfit had tired me out. Luckily I had time for a nap before beautifying myself and meeting at the house for dinner.

The guys cleaned up while I napped so when I awoke I had the bathroom to myself. I took my time and luxuriated in the fact that I could feel everything I was doing. I finally came out of my room in my new duds and stopped in my tracks when I saw the guys. Wow, what a good looking group. It's no wonder girls were jealous of me. Gosh, they could be in that new men's magazine…GQ. I went back to my room, grabbed the camera and made them pose while I whipped off some shots until we had to go. It was a quick jaunt over the bridge to Bridges restaurant on Granville Island.

Adam's dad's company had developed and built Granville Island. What had started out as an industrial site under the south end of the Granville street bridge had been converted into a marina with a high end arts community and a large public market. There was a still a concrete plant right between an arts college and a big theatre, but although the water still wasn't safe to swim in, it would be in a few years as sea life covered up the industrial waste dump.

I was glad Ace was with us as he was in the process of finishing up his university degree in commercial architecture. His minor was in business administration. I felt he and Geoff would have lots to talk about if things got awkward.

We took two cars, Adam's Z280 and Danny's Mustang, and arrived just on time. I was really nervous. I had only met Geoff once and his wife not at all, and these people had just spent a quarter of a million dollars on me. What must they think of me? A young girl with a knife wound dating their son the wealthy, golden boy.

I should let him go, I thought suddenly, and following that I was going to be sick but we were walking up the stairs. I stopped suddenly wanting to run away. *I can't face it.* And the negative spiral of thoughts burst through me in a violent and unending wave.

"Montana, what is it? Are you okay?" Adam asked with concern in his eyes. "Are you in pain? We can leave if you're not up to this, I'll take you home right now."

Oh god, why did he have to take such good care of me? What did I ever do to deserve this type of guy?

"Adam, I feel like I'm going to be sick I am so nervous. I don't deserve you and they are going to know it, you are so high above me in every way. The first thing they are going to say to you the moment they get you alone is what the hell are you thinking son, this girl is a loser."

He looked me in the eye and said, "Just remember that they go to the bathroom and shop and eat and everything else just like you do and they were young once too. It will be okay. As far as everything else you said, don't be ridiculous. That's just your fear talking. Do I look like the kind of guy that would date someone so low?" he said with a smile and a twinkle in his eye.

That made me smile. Of course he wouldn't. With a small pearl of new found confidence I finished the stairs and used every ounce of energy to sashay over to the table. His parents had arrived ahead of us and were already seated at the table. Adam did the introductions. They knew Danny already so he sat down beside Liza, Ace sat down beside Geoff, which left me with Alex and Adam. Perfect. I hated formalities, I was like a duck out of water. Give me a crowd where I could lose myself. That was my comfort zone.

I took a few photos while they all yacked. Observing them was making me feel more comfortable. Clearly Liza looked at Danny as another son. They were engaged in a conversation that had her laughing while Alex, grinning, was tuned into their conversation. Geoff and Ace were talking business which grabbed Adam's attention, leaving me free to observe.

Liza finally turned to me and started asking me questions about my recent 'accident'. I didn't know what Adam had said so I caught his eye and he nodded his head ever so slightly. They knew, so I may as well fess up. I told her the story of Mercy and how she had infiltrated our lives. At some point everyone else at the table stopped talking and listened.

I went right to the beginning of the first day we met, our time at the beach and Adam's observation of her, everything. I finished the same time as the main course. I could see Geoff come to some type of conclusion in his head and Liza looked seemed to look at me differently than when I'd first sat down. I didn't know what that meant, I simply noticed.

Over dessert the conversations shifted to Ace and school and career. Geoff used Ace as an example of the type of industrious young man our province needed more of. I could feel Adam tense, obviously Geoff took every opportunity to share his thoughts on his only child being an artist instead of a business man.....

I cut in, "Excuse me Geoff, when was the last time you were in Adam's apartment?" Adam gripped my knee as if to say shut up. Geoff said it had been a while so I sang Adam's praises until long after dessert. Not just his talent and his work but his business acumen and his sensitivity. The way he could put into layman's terms the legalities of my father's will and help us all deal with his death, and his astounding ability to connect and network with artists and business people alike and close the gap between them academically and socially.

I ended with saying that Adam was such an amazing blend of both his parents' talents that they both must be equally proud. Liza was beaming the entire time; Geoff gave me a grudging hmmph, but smiled at me. He winked at Adam and said," Good luck son, you have a fire cracker there," and he chuckled as he held up his glass in a toast. "To Mo, and her remarkable recovery."

Over coffee, when everyone but Adam and I were talking, he and I had a moment. As I looked at his beautiful chiseled face I knew in that moment that I truly loved him. Not the "Oh, I love you!" that you feel when you date someone that you click with and have fun, but the love that could last all my life. I leaned into him so only he could hear. "I love you. You are the greatest guy in the world." He looked at me and said, "Thanks. I love you too, brat."

It was finally time to leave and Geoff wanted to pay but Ace wouldn't let him. It was our thanks for all of their help. Ace did a great job of making them feel like they had done a great and noble thing. When we were leaving Liza gave me a hug, "It was a pleasure to meet you Montana, and I know now why it's your face all over my son's room." She winked at me and then they were gone. I think we all had a sigh of relief when they left.

"Guys, look at us, we're looking pretty sharp.

Let's go party." Danny said.

"Ace, if it's okay with you, I'm taking Montana back to my place. She needs to rest." Adam scooped me up in his arms before I fell over from exhaustion.

"Adam," Ace said. "I really need to thank you for all you did. You are one in a million and you gave my sister something that no one else could, and for that I will be forever grateful." He gave Adam the kind of hug he only gives to his family, with me sandwiched in the middle.

When he let go they were both kind of teary, and so were the rest of us. "Okay, enough teary stuff you guys. Let's go," Danny said. They left and Adam and I went back to his place..

"Adam, can you grab me a t-shirt? I need to get out of this stuff." I took everything off while he went to his dresser and when he came back he was holding a gift. He gave it to me with a mischievous grin and I opened it. I pulled out a white silk nighty, low cut and billowy through the skirt. I put it on and it felt like a second skin slightly cool and sensuous. "Mmmmm, thank you," I sighed, "this feels amazing."

"Thank *you,*" he said, "it looks as good as I thought it would. You look positively delicious Mo."

"Adam, I want to have sex. It has been months. Please, let's have sex and fall asleep and stay in bed all day tomorrow."

"Okay," he said, "but we have something to deal with first."

My stomach dropped. *Damn, he is going to do what he said when he first came back.* I was hoping he would be so caught up in the victory of me walking that he would have let go of his promise that I was in trouble with him for breaking my word.

We sat down in the living room, and for the next 45 minutes he lectured me on what keeping your word meant and how he expected me to be accountable to that in the future. He actually had me crying and feeling guilty because everything he said was accurate. Then he did something that only Ace and Danny had ever done and not in several years, and never like this. He placed me over his lap and spanked me for a good while, but he was kind to my spine. He wasn't wailing away on me heavily, he very deliberately peeled up my nighty and brought a bright rosy sheen to the skin on my butt. It was like he knew just how hard to hit me to make it sting but not thump me in any way.

I didn't fight it; I just let the guilt of my actions wash away. When he was done I was on fire as he carried me to his room. I felt new. Free. Guilt free. And with nothing hanging over our heads, and nothing to hold us back, we had sex. The most passionate and carefree sex ever. Afterwards, I slept for 12 hours straight and awoke to breakfast in bed.

There was a "gift" with breakfast. Exercise clothes. Ugh. I would continue with my therapy to keep moving towards a full recovery.

Soon after our celebratory dinner school began. Ace had a few months left of university and the pressure was on to choose a company. Offers continued to come in but none of them had felt right yet. Alex and I were in our last year of high school and looking forward to graduating. Danny and Adam had a downtown warehouse space and spent a lot of time there putting together their first show. Danny was working part time at the Vancouver Art Gallery and Adam was doing some work with the UBC museum.

Adam had an investor who was sponsoring their first show and they were busy being seen in the art and business community. The papers frequently had articles and pictures of them at different events, and often I was in them. Two really good looking artists creating their first show captured the hearts of many Vancouverites.

Spending time in the warehouse, I got a lot more insight into the type of artists they were, the similarities and their differences. They both captured similar qualities in their art but their styles were so different from each other.

Adam seemed to paint the realistic feeling or emotion of a scene through recognizable figures and objects while Danny interpreted the life energy and tended to be more abstract in his work. They complemented each other well. Teaming them up for a show was a good thing.

Alex and Otter were doing really great; Alex was writing all the material now and had taken over the bookings. I was still rebuilding my body and balance and relearning many things I had taken for granted.

I decided to go back to dance for therapeutic purposes. The doctors had recommended dance and suggested I give yoga a try also. Slowly, I was repairing the damage that had been done to my body. For right then, that was enough. I liked having that inner quietude as we moved into the autumn season, and I felt at peace.

Danny met someone at the museum and he brought her home for dinner so we could all meet her; her name was Jaimie and she was very sweet and very into art. She was working towards being an art dealer. Danny was completely absorbed by this girl, he watched every move she made and seemed awed every time she opened her mouth. He never noticed the rest of us rolling our eyes when he gazed at her.

I invited her to come out to see the band play that weekend and she said she would love to, that she loved music. So, Friday night Ace and Kristine, Danny and Jaimie, and Adam and I went out to see the guys. I had not seen them play since the night I was stabbed and it all felt very surreal. I kept waiting for Mercy to come walking in or someone to stick something in me.

For the last set, Tim asked me if I would play. I looked at Ace to see what he would say.

"If you want to play then go ahead. It's your choice, Montana." I kissed him hard on the cheek and he turned beet red.

"It's been a while, I probably suck."

Tim laughed," Montana even on your worst day you could never suck, you're a natural."

I looked to Adam, he nodded encouragingly. He always felt I should be playing, not twiddling my thumbs as he called it. I guess I'd been twiddling them a lot lately. So for the last set I went up to the stage and Tim took my place at the table. Otter gave me a big grin, I grinned back. I had missed this. I looked to Alex. He nodded his head in acknowledgment of me, of us and then we began.

As soon as I started to play I connected instantly with Alex and Otter, and we played a powerful set. Our energy soared and so did my spirits. The three of us were in sync and we gave off this incredible sound. I felt power, elation and desire well up inside and I felt like energy was pouring out of my arms and down my drum sticks.

When we were done we got some great applause. I looked at Alex and smiled and Otter and I high-fived each other like we had so many times before. I came back to the table and Jaimie was really enthusiastic about our playing. "Why aren't you the drummer?" She asked.

"I uh, well I, um, used to be, but I haven't played with them for a while."

"Montana, I can tell it's your passion. You are very good, and very good with them. You guys are tight."

"She's the best" Otter added. I smiled at him.

"Excuse me, all that excitement has me needing the bathroom." I had to get out of there, until I picked up those sticks I had forgotten how much I loved to play. I had been so busy learning to walk that I had just not thought about anything else.

Playing woke me up inside somehow. Like being transported to another place.

When I came back Adam gave me a big hug, "You rocked it sweet heart."

"Thanks," I said, "and thanks for being so encouraging, it felt amazing."

Throughout the rest of the night I would catch Jaimie staring at me and I wondered what she thought of the tough girl with the stab wounds. Danny had filled her in when I had gone to the bathroom. The girl whose rich boyfriend had saved her kind of sounded like a fairy tale when I looked at it from a newcomer's perspective.

I really didn't care what anyone thought. I just hoped that whatever it was wouldn't reflect badly on Danny as he clearly was in love with her. When we were leaving the club, Jaimie approached me.

"Montana, I just wanted to say, you are a great drummer and I think you should reconsider playing. Danny told me what happened to you and I have to say that is one of the wildest stories 1 have heard, your family is very ... *colourful*," she said with a grin.

I grinned back. I liked her. "Well, as long as you don't scare easy," I said. "My brother really likes you and I hope nothing he said about me scared you off."

"On the contrary," she replied, " I find you all fascinating and for the record I like your brother a lot too. He is a really great guy."

"He is the best guy. Whoever lands him is lucky. Soooo if someone ever messed with him, the rest of his family would take it very personally," I added with enough ice in my voice to make my meaning clear.

She smiled, "I get your meaning and I promise not to hurt your brother."

"I've said my peace. So as long as we get each other, then it's all good. By the way Jaimie, I'm pulling for you. I think you're a great fit."

We laughed. "What are you two talking about?" Danny asked as he came over to us. I looked at Jaimie and said, "Politics." We had a good laugh at that. Poor Danny, he just looked confused which had us laughing even harder.

"Oh Danny, you're a real card, you know that?" I said, tears running from my eyes now as the joke continued to build for Jaimie and I.

"A wild card, or a joker?" He answered. I had to cut him some slack, the poor dear.

"A winner, man. Always a winner." We separated in the parking lot each to his own vehicle, "Have fun kids!" I yelled to Jaimie and Danny as I was getting into Adams car. I could hear Jaimie laughing as Danny closed her door, and saw him send me a look that said *we'll talk later*.

Ace came over to the car as we were about to pull out, "Are you home tonight?" he asked.

"Do you want me to be?" I asked back. "I was going to Adam's but I can go home if you want."

"No, no that's fine. I just wanted to know your plans, I don't see you much these days." I thought about that for a minute. Adam had replaced him with respect to helping me and I hadn't really spent any time with him in the last month.

"Ace, why don't we go and have breakfast on Sunday together and go do something fun -- like letting me kick your butt at basketball?"

"You're on." he grinned. "Sunday then," he said as he walked back over to Kristine.

For the rest of our weekend together, Adam and I walked and took pictures and... did other things. We even did some yoga. He said he learned some as a kid watching "Kareen," some tall blond woman on CBC, the Canadian national tv. Station. So, when the doctors recommended it for my recovery, he found us some classes to attend.

Adam and I went to some really cool yoga classes and I started to enjoy the benefits of regular practice. Adam drove me home Sunday morning and Ace and I went for breakfast.

"Hey big brother. So, what's up? What's new, what's going on?"

The waitress came over and took our order. I ordered the 'everything' breakfast. For some reason I was really hungry. Ace got the same.

"Hmm, what's new..." he said after the waitress had gone to get us coffee. "Well, let's see. Kristine and I have decided to call it quits."

That news had me sitting straight, "Why? You guys are such a great couple."

"Our interests are taking us in different directions right now... and in truth, we have not spent a lot of time around each other lately."

I felt guilty. "It's probably my fault. I don't think a lot of women would want to date a guy who is saddled down with a teenage brat. I could talk to her."

He smiled, "No Mo, it's not you. For the first time ever I am just kind of living my own life. Danny and Alex don't need me and you have Adam, so my time has not had the same constraints that it has in the past."

"Ace, does it bother you that Adam stepped in and did all that he did? Because-- to be honest -- it was weird for me to see him like that, you know, in that kind of commanding role. It's always been you. That sounds weird doesn't it?"

"No, not at all." he laughed, "And Mo, you should get used to it. I think Adam is going to be a fine boyfriend/babysitter," he said, laughing again. I gave him a disgusted look.

"No. I didn't feel bad," Ace continued, "just for the first time ever I felt out of my league. I couldn't fix it and that really bothered me. The fact he could was such a big relief."

"So then, what is the problem with you and Kristine? If it's only a time thing then maybe we should look at changing things around the house. I mean, you have all the responsibility and the rest of us just float in and out of there, maybe we need more of a schedule or something so you can have more freedom." I caught him eyeing me with a smirk so I punched him hard enough to finish my spiel.

"Ace, sometimes I feel really bad that you're the oldest. You didn't pick it and you have so much you are responsible for... and then when I screw up -- because I always do--" he was laughing again as I said that, "life becomes more of a burden to you and I wish it wasn't like that. Although, I still maintain that you're the best dad in the world."

Over breakfast Ace told me about how he was feeling about the different circles that he and Kristine were now traveling in socially. They had both agreed that they should just be friends for a while. He was getting that much closer to the end of school and the intensity was building towards final exams and studying and he needed the time to concentrate on that.

"I also have some decisions to make about *where* I will work," he said, looking down at his plate.

"What do you mean?" I asked. "What decisions?"

"I have been offered some pretty lucrative jobs, but so far all the companies have been in the States. I don't want to move to the U.S."

Holy smokes! I never considered that his work after graduation would take him away. This was all new to me. My face must have said it all because he quickly assured me that he wasn't leaving us, but we may need to move. Or he may work during the week in the States and come home on the weekends so Dan would take over at our house here. I stopped eating. Move? Where would we move?

We had lived in the same house since Ace was a little boy, it was our home. How could he even think of leaving it? I looked at him, really taking him in. *Poor guy,* I thought. No wonder he had seemed so gloomy.

"Ace, what do you want after graduation? What would be the perfect situation for you?" He thought for a minute.

"I'd like to stay here and have you and Alex finish up school at King George. Then we can say all the Stanford kids graduated from K.G." That sounded pretty lame to me and my face showed it. He explained, "I don't think pulling you out halfway to grad is good, and with only a few months left I'm sure Dan could handle it if need be. I would like to stay local so I could be here for you guys. Who knows? Danny could be back in Europe at some point or New York, so someone needs to be here." This was closer to the truth and my biggest bro was starting to speak from his heart.

"I want to get in with a company where I can make a difference. An expanding firm that needs help getting rooted, or maybe an established company that needs re-branding or help finding a new direction. A more earth-friendly direction, that kind of thing." My wheels were turning. Didn't Adam's dad talk to Ace about that very thing at dinner the other night? I knew that Geoff was someone who could appreciate my big brother. He seemed to have a lot of respect for what he had accomplished already. I resolved to talk to Adam about it later that night. Ace and I left the restaurant and went for a walk around Stanley Park instead of playing basketball. We stopped at Ceperley Park to play on the swings, then we went down to the beach and had a water fight. We sat down against the logs to dry off in the sun. We'd had a fine day, the two of us just being goofy together. It had been a long time since that had happened and it was so cool to watch the worry lines leave his face.

Danny and Jaimie were in the kitchen making dinner when we arrived home. Adam was on his way to join us for dinner so I headed off to the shower to clean up. Before leaving, I gave Ace a big hug and thanked him for the day. "I had an awesome time big bro," I said, as I squeezed him as tightly as I could.

"Me too Peanut, but I feel bad burdening you with my stuff."

"Hey it's cool. I have no problem with your stuff, and I know it will all work out perfectly for you." I left before my face gave away my thoughts and jumped in the shower to rinse off. I finished changing just as Adam arrived. We were just sitting down to dinner on the back porch when the doorbell rang. Alex went to answer it and came back with Chrissie.

She looked radiant as she sat down to dinner. I smiled at her and said hi. "Sorry I'm late," she said, looking at Alex. I watched Ace at the head of the table. He surveyed the scene and I wondered if he and I were having similar thoughts. This moment seemed so fresh and full, another to preserve in our memory banks.

I was often the observer of these events instead of actively participating. I loved people watching and getting these opportunities with family and friends was great. Last time we had done this was just before my suicide attempt when Adam and I had spent the night under the stars and he told me about the different constellations. All had been well. It seemed like a lifetime ago….

"Montana. Montana…."

"Yes?"

"I'm coming for you Montana. We are coming for you…" Suddenly, my eyes appeared lifeless and dead before me. Then my entire face appeared and it was speaking at me in a voice I could not recognize…. *"We're coming for you…."* Maggots began to pour out of my mouth and eyes and ears and my mind screamed--

"Leave me alone!" My outside voice must have joined in.

"Mo, honey, wake up. It's just you and me, it's okay." Adam was there.

"Adam, it was horrible. Something bad is going to happen, I can feel it. Something evil is on my trail and it haunts me in my sleep."

I told Adam about the dream and how it was always the same, the dead lifeless eyes, but this time was different. It was the first time I had talked to myself and it wasn't me, not my voice. Very creepy. He held me tight and his warmth took me into a deep sleep. Red eyes forgotten, I abandoned myself to nothingness….

Chapter 5

The next morning, I talked to Adam about Ace's situation and asked him how he felt about talking to his dad about hiring Ace for his company.

"He's gone until Wednesday but I promise I will talk to him when he gets back. Besides," he added, "you're not going anywhere. You belong with me."

Just prior to Halloween we received the good news that Ace was hired by Geoff's company and would start December 1st. He questioned me and didn't believe me when I said I had nothing to do with his job. Whatever thoughts he had about my interference, he came home from his first day bubbling over with his thoughts on the company, how great it was, and all the people he had met.

Christmas was around the corner and I was excited again. I love Christmas, but last year I had been in my depression and had not even noticed Christmas. Dad died, Ace freaked out, and I attempted suicide. Fortunately, Danny fished me out of the ocean before I could drown myself.

This year something was in the air like a promise of great things to come which put me in a celebratory mood. I went all out on decorations and made it my mission to put everyone who came across my path in a festive mood.

Christmas holidays arrived so with no school I slept in and shopped and wished I had more money. With no gig playing my stash was dwindling fast. If I got desperate I knew one of my brothers would give me a loan, but still it kind of irked me that they all had incomes and I didn't. I needed a job.

I asked Ace what he thought about me getting a job. He said if I needed money to ask him. That seemed odd since the Stanford kids were all about making their own money, their own way. So I asked Dan the same question and he gave me the same answer. Now I was curious, what was actually going on? Why did they not want me to work?

"Guilt." Alex said. "Ace feels bad that you gave up the drums, Dan feels bad that he wasn't here. So they are babying you, Mo."

"I want to play. I miss it so badly. I'm fully recovered. If I can't get a job then they should let me play. I have proven that the attacks on me were premeditated and had nothing to do whatsoever with random guys wanting to get their hands on me."

"Are you ready to come back? Otter wants you and I want you. I feel like we're treading water without you."

"Hell ya, and the fact that I'm not playing with you guys seems ridiculous."

Alex reflected. "I have a plan. Just give me a bit of time, until after Christmas. Something is in the works and if it goes through, Ace can't say no."

"I trust you, Alex. I can wait. Besides, Christmas is coming and for some reason I am especially excited this year." I'd thought a lot about what to give everyone this year. It was important to me that the gifts reflected how I felt and saw the most important people in my life.. I blew my budget on the first present I bought for Adam. I couldn't resist the flat gold chain I saw in People's jewelers. It would look amazing on his always tanned skin.

I also had this super-hot picture of him that I had taken up in the woods on one of our trips. I had it blown up and framed. Next, I went to Long and McQuade, Otter had told me about a guitar that Alex had been eyeing up. I asked Danny if he wanted to go in on it together. He had agreed as he was at a loss of what to buy for him anyway.

I instructed Otter that it was his job to make sure Alex didn't buy it when they went to Long and McQuade together later that day to look around.

I found a leather jacket that I knew Danny had to have, because he would look hot in it, so I bought it for him. I also framed one of my pictures of him and dad from his last visit. Ace was the toughest to buy for as he never wanted anything, or at least never told anyone if he did. I wanted his gift to be special and really personal.

I decided I needed Adam's help with this one so I gave him a group of photos of Ace starting with when he was little right up to this year and I had Adam draw them in a collage. In the center, Adam superimposed a poem that I had written for Ace. It was beautiful.

Adam had caught every nuance of Ace, his drawings were better than the photos, and the poem was perfect for the center. It would a gift from both of us. Finally, Otter. We had exchanged little gifts every year but I felt like Otter was family. He would be a part of our lives forever because of the band and the bond we shared.

Alex and I ended up buying a new bass case and strings for him together. Our family had received an invitation for a Christmas Eve dinner at the Northrop's. When we arrived, the house looked amazing, as festive as you could possibly imagine. It was literally right out of a magazine; Canadian

Home magazine had done a write up on the family and even mentioned Adam and Danny's show in the spring.

Inside, the house had been professionally decorated and was as gorgeous as the outside winter wonderland they had created. Every surface in the formal dining space was covered with amazing decor and delicious appetizers. Liza had outdone herself.

Geoff immediately stole Ace and took him over to the fireplace. I grinned to see him so happily engaged. Liza asked me many questions and regaled me with humorous tales of Adam's childhood. She was a gracious woman, kind and sensitive, a lot like Adam. You could see her influence in the more traditional aspects of Adams personality and his steadfast loyalty.

Adam came over and kissed my hand, "I've been thinking about you all day."

I grinned, "Oh really, and what have you been thinking?"

"Nothing I can say out loud," he laughed. I punched him in the arm, "You're terrible," I laughed.

"Adam, before we leave tonight can we grab a few minutes alone so I can give you your Christmas present?"

"Oh I see, you bought me a Christmas present. And here I thought you were just going to wrap yourself up with a big red bow for me to untie. I don't have yours yet." His eyes twinkled in merriment..

"Okay, Mr. Sarcastic. I see you're in fine form this evening. I'm usually the bratty one, remember? If you're not careful I'll be the one chasing you around."

He just laughed and put his arm around me with a fading smirk. "Promises, promises. You know me so well. Let's go mingle." Finally, it was time to be seated for dinner. I was almost completely full just from the appetizers.

I observed everyone. We were divided by social class and money, yet sitting at the table we all seemed to fit. Maybe Adam had been right all along. We all put on our pants on one leg at a time. We all go to the bathroom the same way, pretty much. Social standing was no issue here. Apparently, I had always thought money meant more than it did when it came to judging people.

Alex drove the conversation in his little group, natural entertainer that he was. Socially speaking, Danny was the quietest of us all but had been around this type of environment before because of his friendship with Adam, so he was clearly comfortable.

Ace was seated to Geoff's right. Ha! I thought, his right hand man. In that moment I saw Ace years from now in Geoff's position, doing what he always wanted to do, being in charge.

My focus turned to Adam. As I watched him chatting with his parents his left hand remained on my thigh. Adam was always touching me. No matter where we were, there was always a physical connection. I sighed, and wondered for probably the thousandth time what he saw in me.

After our meal I strolled around and took pictures of everyone. Liza approached me when I stopped to admire a black and white photo gallery on one huge wall.

"Montana, Adam has shown me some of your photos. You have a great eye. Have you considered working in photo journalism?"

I said that I hadn't. She proceeded to tell me about her career in photo journalism and how she gave it up when she met Geoff to help him launch his company.

"Are those yours?" I asked, nodding towards the black and whites. She nodded. "They are beautiful, Mrs. Northrop."

"Call me Liza, please. Listen. If this is something you're interested in, I could help you."

I promised to consider it and I thanked her for the invitation tonight. I handed her a present for her and Geoff and asked her to open it. I was nervous. I didn't know what she would say. It was a photo of the three of them at dinner the night we'd met.

The picture showed them in a genuinely warm moment and I had Adam make a frame for it. She gave me a hug. "Thank you, Montana. It's lovely." I blushed and she excused herself to go and show Geoff. I continued looking at the various photos on the walls some of them were of Adam.

I felt a familiar arm wrap around me. He leaned in. "You're a hit," he whispered in my ear.

"Huh? With who?" I was caught up in my musings so I had no idea what he was talking about.

"My mom. She loves you and she is over there right now showing everyone the picture you took of my family."

I blushed, "Well, I'm glad she likes it. Her work is amazing. She asked me if I would be interested in a career in photo journalism."

That surprised him. "Wow. My mom doesn't talk about her career." He gazed through me, as he did from time to time when assessing me in his Adam way. "I'm surprised that she shared with you about who she used to be. What did you tell her?"

"Well, I told her I would think about it. I love photography and I'm grateful that you showed me how to compose and take a picture, but you know where my heart lies."

He nodded and kissed me on my forehead, "You. The evening is winding down. Since you're not wearing a bow, I want to see what is."

"Not here. Let's go upstairs to your apartment." I caught Alex's eye and he raised his glass as we slipped away.

First, I gave Adam the photo, which he loved, and then I gave him the chain. He put it on and just as I thought, it looked amazing on him. He wrapped me in a warm embrace and gave me a kiss. "You must have broken the bank."

"Whatever. You always tell me that money is a tool and to be used as such. I used mine to buy the love of my life a Christmas present. It's only money, Adam."

He looked ready to throw me on the bed.

"So what did you get me?" I asked. He paused, collected himself, and pulled out an envelope and a small box and asked me to open the box first. I undid the wrapping and opened the box and almost dropped it. Nestled inside was a diamond ring. A big diamond ring. I looked at him shocked. "This isn't an engagement ring is it?"

He laughed, "Why, would you say yes if it was?" I looked him dead in the eye and said, "You know I would. But be serious Adam, what does this ring mean?"

"No. It's not an engagement ring, at least not yet. If it were, I wouldn't have handed it to you in a box. We would be somewhere romantic and I would be on one knee. This is a promise ring, Montana. It is for this hand, but I would like it to be on the other hand. One day, when we are ready."

"Adam, it's too much! I can't take it. I can't even guess at how much this cost." There was that class difference rearing its ugly head in my subconscious, the same voice that said, *"You're not good enough Montana."*

"Really? After what you just said to me about money being a tool, now you're lecturing me? It wasn't as much as you think. Just put it on and see how it looks."

I did put it on and it looked glorious. "It is so elegant and beautiful."

"Like you," he said with a wink. "Okay, now open the envelope."

I opened the envelope. Inside was another envelope and inside of that was plane tickets. They had the date of June 21st on them. I looked at him confused, and asked, "What are these for?"

"Europe," he said.

"You're going to Europe again? After what happened the last time you left me... you don't really want a repeat of all that, do you?" I said half-jokingly.

"No, I never want a repeat of what happened. That is why you're coming with me so I can keep my eye on you."

I looked down at the tickets and sure enough my name was on one of them. "Are you pulling my leg, is this for real?"

He nodded, clearly enjoying the total and utter shock on my face. I jumped on him, "Really? We are going together, where? Tell me, where we are going?" I closed my eyes and envisioned the places as he said the names…England, Wales, Scotland, France, Italy, Amsterdam, and Spain…

I couldn't believe it. "This is too much. You have to take something back. You know I have a hard time accepting gifts of this magnitude."

"Why do you have such a hard time accepting *gifts of this magnitude*?" That was a good question. Why was it so hard? Because everyone in my family worked so hard for what they had? That was certainly part of it. I thought about gifts I received over the years…I had never been given anything frivolous, only things that would better me or my situation.…

"Um, I think because I was never given gifts that didn't include self-improvement or something specific that I needed. My mom died young, Alex and I were very young and my dad was good with the guy gifts. You know, footballs and those types of things.

But I guess with me he never knew what to get me. So, I would get dance lessons, or Kung Fu classes or something that kept me busy. Never did I receive jewelry or trips or anything that was simply meant for pleasure. I don't even know what to do with gifts like this. It's all so foreign."

He smiled in understanding, "You're so self-sufficient in so many ways I often forget you lost your mom so young. You're right, that situation would make a big impact on how you receive or in your case struggle with receiving. Just so you know, I can't take anything back. So, you will just have to accept these tokens of my love for you."

Returning downstairs. Alex noticed the ring right away and gave a whistle. "Nice hardware there sis." "That's not all" I grinned, "I'm going to Europe! I am so excited."

I showed him the tickets for Europe; he whistled again. "Wow, your Adam sure knows how to give gifts." I nodded my agreement.

It was time to head home. I said goodbye to Geoff first. I had not spoken with him all evening. He noticed the ring as he lifted my hand to kiss it. Our eyes met for the briefest of moments. I was worried that his look would be one of disapproval. Instead, he seemed genuinely pleased.

I was relieved. The man intimidated me. He was very powerful and confident, like Ace would be in another 20 years. Liza noticed the ring and grabbed my hand for a better look. Her response was warm. "I see you received your Christmas present." I blushed and nodded my head. "It suits you perfectly. Wear it in good health...and keep it safe the rest of the time."

I thanked her, kissed Adam goodbye, and our clan left. On the way home, Alex and Ace took turns looking at the ring and giving me a bad time, teasing me and trying to get a rise out of me. I was too excited and didn't pay attention. I stared at the ring. I never imagined that I would be wearing such a large diamond.

The ring was a promise ring. That meant he was committed to marrying me one day! The tickets would change my perspective on life. I had barely been out of the West End and now I was going to see dozens of cities in a dozen countries! I couldn't have been more thrilled.

"Ace, did you enjoy your evening? Was your time with Geoff advantageous?"

"You bet." He continued, "the job is getting more interesting and has far more to offer than I could have ever imagined." He paused, then asked me if I knew what he wanted for Christmas. "No Ace, what do you want for Christmas?"

"To know if you were the little bird who told Mr. Northrop that I was looking for a local company to hire on with." Alex sat silent as stone. He knew, not because I told him, he just knew like he knew all things I thought or did.

"Does it really matter Ace?"

"Yes it matters. It matters to me," he answered a little too sternly.

"Okay. Well then, the answer is yes and no. When you and I had gone for breakfast and had our talk--I remembered how impressed Mr. Northrop had been with you at my recovery dinner—and... I asked Adam to find out if he was looking for someone and if he could get your name added to the list of people they were looking at. Adam told me after you were hired that you were the best candidate by far and his dad was really glad he got you. So, you did all that on your own, bro."

When we arrived home, he gave me a hug. "I'm mad at you, but I forgive you. Just let me worry about my own life from now on. I was going to go and talk to him anyway."

"Well, everything worked out then. So, how can

you be mad?" I concluded. Alex snorted behind me. Apparently, I was having a blond moment.

"I am a man in charge of my own destiny. I like to make things happen on my own, without interference from my baby sister. Don't get me wrong, I appreciate it, but that is the last time you get in my business, okay?"

"Okay," I responded.

He gave me the look. "I am serious, no more interference with my life young lady, promise me."

I did promise and this had taught me a valuable lesson…that men wanted to be men, even if they made stupid choices they wanted to be allowed to be who and what they were. Ace was a pioneer, he would pave his own way. I got the point that in future, trying to manipulate his future would be a waste of my time.

I didn't get much sleep that night. The nightmares were strong and kept replaying. I woke in a sweaty tangled heap. Getting up, I put on the coffee and showered before waking up the rest of the crew.

I contemplated my nightmares. Why were they so persistent and what was I so afraid of? When I had attempted suicide I'd had to undergo mandatory therapy sessions. The subconscious was mentioned a lot. I knew something was wrong with the amount of wrong that had already happened in my short life, but determining the trigger for this current haunting was proving near impossible.

I knew rooted deep inside of me was fear. I could feel it like a nagging tooth ache. The nightmares came from the fear, or caused the fear? I was unsure. With Mercy being tried in adult court, I had nothing to fear from her. I couldn't think of who else would be after me, or wanted to hurt me but there was a pit inside. A warning that whatever she had begun was not yet finished....

I poured everyone's coffee and set them down on the coffee table. Then I went and got my soaker gun and filled it up. The little darlings were all tucked in their beds. Well, Santa was long gone! I opened Dan's door first and shot him in the face until he rolled off the far side of his bed. Then I raced for Alex's room and repeated what I had done to Dan. Ace was last and I stood in the door frame, not wanting to get too close to a sleeping bear.

I shot until he was roaring. Then, I hid my gun under my bed and sat down in the living room with a coffee in my hands. They came stumbling out of their rooms looking for the water gun bandit. "Good morning my lovely brothers. Merry Christmas. Please sit, as coffee is served."

They looked confusedly at each other. Ace was drying his head with a towel and stripping off his shirt. He'd gotten the worst of it which made Alex and Danny chuckle. Normally Ace would have erupted but seeing as it was Christmas and I had clearly diffused their anger with my charm, they sat and we drank our coffee with little chatter. After coffee Ace got up and put on Christmas music and we opened our presents. Ace handed out his gifts first just like dad used to do. I got a super slick backpack for Europe filled with everything a girl could possibly need for traveling.

"Adam told you." He winked. I gave him a tight hug of thanks.

Ace gave Danny an Armani suit. It was for the art opening coming up in March. Danny was a little shocked. "Holy Ace! You save any money for yourself?" Ace just smiled and beckoned Alex to follow him.

Alex's present was outside so we went out on the porch to see it. On the street was a dirt bike with all the trimmings. Ace said dad had wanted Alex to have one so he made sure dad's request was granted. Alex was beside himself as he went and sat on it. He was so excited he kept repeating, "Oh man, this is so cool."

We went back inside and it was my turn to hand out my gifts. Danny and I gave Alex his present together, the guitar, and he was thrilled. " I have been eyeing this up for months. Thanks you guys, this really rocks."

Next, I gave Danny the picture and then the jacket. He got a little teary eyed when he saw the picture of him and dad. "You sure take great pictures, Montana. Thanks, I really love it."

He tried on the jacket and as I had thought it looked totally hot and fit him like a glove. He said he was never taking it off.

Last on the list was Ace. I handed him his present with a trembling heart. He was either going to love it or hate it. He took off the wrapping and didn't say a word. His stillness was like a beacon. Danny and Alex got up to see the gift.

"Wow," were the only words spoken for at least a minute. Then Dan commented on Adam's contribution which made me pipe up.

"It is a joint gift from both of us. Ace, what do you think? Do you like it?"

He looked up at me. "I love it. I'm going to hang it in my office so I can see it all the time. You spent a lot of time on this gift and it is the most amazing thing anyone has ever, ever given me," he put it down and gave me a big hug. "Thanks, I really mean it," he whispered.

Danny was next up. He gave me a drawing of me and Adam, a beautiful drawing that I couldn't wait to hang up in my room. He bought me a leather bound journal and said it was for writing down things on my trip. For Ace he had painted a piece of art for his new office and to Alex he gave a stained glass piece that was about 6 feet in length of an almost life-sized Alex wailing on the guitar. That was really cool.

Alex was last. He gave Danny a video from the time Dan was a little boy until now. He had stuff on there from Europe that Adam had given him. We watched it later that day and laughed watching little Danny, then bigger Danny, and finally the now Danny.

For Ace he had written a song and recorded it on video. A dedication to him, a song that Alex had written just after dad died but had not played publicly yet. Its debut was on the video and Ace and the four of us were the first ones to hear and see it. So powerful was Alex playing an acoustic, sitting on a stool in a recording studio somewhere, that we were pretty teary by the end of it.

For me, Alex made a video of me playing at all our gigs. I don't know how he had gotten the footage as I was unaware of being filmed, but I was mesmerized. I had never seen myself play. I finally understood what Alex and Otter had been saying, that it was one thing to feel it, but quite another to witness it.

There I was loud and proud. A female rocker, a drummer goddess. I was kick ass. Ha! I had no idea how good I really was. When it was done I stood and looked at my brothers and my attitude was in full force. "Are you kidding me? I had no idea how good I was. Ace, how could you make me give that up? That is who I am, what I am and I'm going back no matter what anybody says."

I didn't care if I ruined Christmas. I left the room, then came back. "I am going for a walk. I will be home on time to cook dinner."

Ace was talking but I wasn't listening, I slammed the door and headed for the beach. The Christmas carol ships were in the harbor and there was morning singing. It was beautiful. I sat on a huge log and listened until they were done. I was about to leave when Alex joined me.

"Hey sis, my plan worked."

"What are you saying, Alex? That you used Christmas to get me pissed off enough that I would demand to play?"

"Yep." I laughed. I laughed so hard that I fell off the log and onto the soft sand. Alex joined me and we laughed for quite a while.

"Alex, what happened after I left, what did Ace say?"

"It wasn't Ace, it was Danny. Your valiant knight of a brother told Ace in no uncertain terms that you were coming back to the band. That keeping you from it was ridiculous."

"So, what did Ace say to that?"

"Well, you weren't there. So, he didn't need to save face like he feels the need to when you're around, so he asked me what I thought."

"And?"

"Well, what do you think? I made the video for you on purpose to get them to see the truth. So, of course I said I agreed with Dan."

"You're brilliant, brother. Thank you. No one could have given me a better gift." I sat in my own glow for a while.

"Mo, what's with the nightmares?" One thing about my family, we don't beat around the bush. I saw his concern so I put my arm around him and let him in.

"I don't know, bro. I feel fine you know, like the everyday me is great. I guess down in my gut I feel something is unfinished. I don't know. It's just a feeling-- and the dreams-- I think they are a message but they are so brutal and frightening."

He put his arm around me and we sat in each other's embrace staring at the sea. That is how our brothers found us an hour or so later. They sat down and joined us. Somewhere there was Christmas music and it lent to the magical feel of the day. I had willing partners to make a kick-ass dinner and I only had to dodge one glass of water that was aimed at my head and ended up hitting Adam who had no idea what that was all about. I explained it to him later and I think he sort of understood by the time the holidays were over.

I was back in the saddle on the drums for New Year's Eve. Tim said he was relieved because it never really felt right for him. I had a bit of catching up to do but as I continued to practice with the band and on my own it didn't take long. I was so happy to be playing in a band again the time just flew by. With no hard feelings, Alex hooked Tim up with Cole's band and it turned out to be an easy fit for them.

A couple of months went by. I stayed home most nights to practice in the garage even after practicing with the band. I saw Adam on weekends and we had some blissful days and the occasional night. Next up was Alex's and my seventeenth birthday. We had a birthday bash and Alex announced that we would be participating the weekend after next in a battle of the bands. There was a chance to pick up an agent or win a record deal.

We were so busy in the following weeks preparing for the competition that I didn't see Adam at all. Going directly from school to rehearsal every day I learned ten new songs in the same number of days and a 10-minute medley that Alex had created for us to finish our set.

I was struggling with insecurity towards the end of the second week with the battle coming up.... That night at practice Alex let me have it.

"Montana you're playing great!" Otter nodded his agreement, "But you need to let go, you're trying too hard. Don't sweat it so much. You have it down, just play and let the music flow. Be the instrument instead of playing the instrument, remember?

So I worked on feeling and letting go, and for the next hour, I got better and better. Then the magical connection took over and I disappeared and we were just an energetic connection producing sounds, and it was cool.

Our gig on Friday was at a huge gymnasium. If we moved forward in the competition we would play at the Pacific Coliseum where five thousand people were expected to attend. I was terrified. Ace changed his plans so he could attend the Saturday night and keep his eye on me. His confidence in us was amazing. His distrust of others, well...I could see his point.

Danny and Adam attended the Friday night as both entourages and body guards. I felt better knowing that they would be there. I was really nervous, almost like the first time we had played together. This battle of the bands was not a traditional contest where there was one winner. Instead, you auditioned and those that were accepted on the Friday went through to Saturday where they would get exposure to a huge crowd and reps from record labels, radio stations, and a host of others who made the music world happen.

When it was our turn I checked my equipment one more time. Danny and Adam were watching us from behind the stage. I turned for a last look and they both gave me big cheesy grins and two thumbs up like Siskel and Ebert, the movie reviewers. I smiled and waved, turned away and felt the necklace I was wearing, the one Ralph had given me for my birthday so long ago. It was my playing necklace I wore for good luck at all my gigs. I said a little prayer to Ralph to give me strength and not let me screw up.

I led in and the next thirty minutes were a blur. I sensed Alex leading us to the medley and then we were done. It was dead silent for what seemed like ten seconds and then the crowd erupted. It was almost scary actually and they yelled for more, just like in the concerts we had attended.

I looked to Alex and Otter. They both wore ear splitting grins. We were given permission to play one more song. We played our dedication song that we had written for Ralph. It was a little slower and brought the energy down a bit for the next act.

As we came off stage, we received high fives from Danny, "You killed it," he said. I walked into Adam's waiting arms and luxuriated for a moment in the hard reality of him. The night had been a victory and I felt elated, relieved, and somehow different. I had a feeling that things would never be the same. We had crossed a line which would forever change us.

My reverie was short-lived as back to reality-- it was time to pack up for tomorrow at the coliseum.

An agent came up to congratulate us on our performance. Adam and Alex took a moment to talk shop while the rest of us loaded our stuff.

Alex was so hyper, I had never seen him so wound up. Adam and Dan brought us home and we had drinks as we discussed the night. The talent we had competed against was good. Some were very good. "You killed it and you guys will win this event." Dan said suddenly.

"You think so?" Alex asked.

"I know so. The crowd loved you," declared Danny.

"What do you think, Montana? How was it for you?" Asked Alex.

"Honestly, I don't remember much. But it felt amazing. I was gone, Alex, totally in the music. The stadium could have been burning down and I wouldn't have noticed."

We all shared a laugh at that, and were still laughing when Ace walked through the door. We had to tell all the stories again. I was exhausted. I felt anesthetized by the few drinks I'd had and was ready for sleep. I signaled to Adam to see if he would be joining me, he rose and said goodnight to everyone.

The next morning Adam and I went out for breakfast. I wanted to talk to him about this agent and the possibility of a contract. "Adam, I don't know what to do. A record deal is a huge opportunity but it will be hard work and it may take me, in fact, I *know* it will take me on the road and as much as I would like that-- I have a lot to stay here for, you know what I mean? I'm nervous. I have never handled the crowd thing well or the adulation that seems to come with success. Alex is a natural and it doesn't bother him or change him. Can you tell me what to do?"

He smiled, "Montana, I wish life were that easy, but you have to find your own path and do what seems right to you. You are seventeen years old. You and Alex have a few months left of school. I don't think there will be any big tours before then but you will have to cross that road when you come to it. Bottom line is, you need to do what is right for you. Who knows? Maybe the guy won't even sign you on. Wait and see what happens before you make any major decisions, okay?"

"Okay, you're right. I'm panicking and I need to chill, but would you still want to be with me if I became some famous drummer? You know, like…well I would be super busy, I think. How do you feel about that?"

"Mo, compared to before Christmas I haven't seen you very much and that hasn't stopped me. I would want you crippled, super famous, rich, or poor, I don't care. And listen, tours aren't the end of the world. I will have art tours and we can certainly follow each other on our down time. You're young. You might decide to be done in 10 years and you'll be wealthy in your own right, no more class distinction," he finished with a gentle smile.

That made a whole lot of sense and went a long way towards making me feel comfortable. I felt ready to embrace the next stage of the journey. Ace and Adam were our traveling companions/private security for the day, and Danny and Jaimie changed their plans to come and see us.

We were scheduled to play two sets of twenty minutes each as the first and last act, which made for a damn long day. But, there was so much excitement in the air it was contagious and my energy felt as electric as Alex's guitar.

Alex didn't want us to give the audience all our high energy stuff at the beginning so we teased them and had only the last two songs from the first set be high powered, and the crowd went nuts. The other bands were good and the last one that played before us was very strong. In another year they would be ready for the big time.

We were on again for our last set and we nailed it. We brought out all the heavy artillery and kicked butt. There was no silence this time, just the crowd going nuts and we ended up doing an extra song just like the night before.

As soon as we got off the stage the agent from last night was there along with several others. Adam and Ace stepped in to help Alex out and the rest of us packed up. Just as we were finishing, Adam, came over and said they would meet us at Bino's 24 hour diner. We had stuff to talk about.

Otter, Danny, Jaimie and I ordered our food and then we waited for Ace, Adam and Alex to meet up and tell us what was happening. We were almost done eating by the time the guys arrived. Alex started in immediately, declining a menu from the waitress. He was way too excited and agitated to eat anything.

"Okay, this is the scoop. There are three different agents who would like us to sign on with their label. We're going to need a lawyer and go in for some interviews, but the bottom line is all three are offering a similar deal, a five year contract. Tours and percentages differ a little with all three but it is a standard contract for new bands so they are all very similar. I feel it will come down to who wants to negotiate the finer points of the contract with us and who offers the most money.

Nothing was said. Alex was grinning and the rest of us were just stunned. I felt my whole life flashing before my eyes and had so many unanswered questions. I got up quickly and ran to the bathroom and threw up. A few minutes later I heard Jaimie calling my name, "Montana, are you okay? Danny sent me in to see how you're feeling."

I came out of the stall and washed my face, leaning on the counter to get my breath. I stood to find Jaimie examining me. How long have you been feeling like this?"

"I don't know. A few minutes."

Jaimie stared me down. "Really? Throwing up?"

That stopped me. I had been feeling weird and thought it was just nerves. "A couple of weeks."

"Are you sure you're not pregnant?"

I gazed at her image in the mirror, by comparison to her calm expression mine was a mask of shock and denial. "No, no, um no, no way, couldn't be."

She hesitated, "There is a nasty flu going around, maybe that is what you have?"

"Probably, I have been tired and achy and randomly throwing up."

"Maybe go and see a doctor if it doesn't go away in a few days."

"Good idea."

Back at the table Adam gave me a look of concern. "Nerves, I think." I volunteered and sat back down beside him. Danny and Jaimie said their goodbyes and left. Alex and Otter were busy debating who they thought was the best label and

Adam and Ace were discussing the legal
ramifications of the deals. I just leaned on Adam
and I guess I fell asleep because he shook me awake
when it was time to go.

"Montana," Alex said, "how can you sleep at a
time like this. Aren't you excited?"

"Hmm, yes I'm excited. Just really tired for some
reason."

Adam helped me into his car. We were just
heading over the bridge when I got a stabbing pain.
I screamed and Adam almost crashed the car. I had
another stabbing pain and then I felt a gush. When I
looked down I was sitting in blood.

Once across the bridge Adam headed straight for
VGH. I moaned like some wounded beast. I hated
looking weak, even in my agony I tried to control
myself. We arrived at the hospital and as Adam was
helping me out of the car I had a slice of pain across
my belly.

I woke up feeling much better. I realized I was in a hospital bed and was curious as to what the pain had been about. Adam's voice floated across the room to me as well as that of a doctor. I opened up my eyes.

"Hey," he said softly, "how are you feeling?"

"Much better. What happened? I thought maybe food poisoning, then when I saw the blood I thought I was getting my period, but that was like nothing I have ever experienced before."

Adam looked sad as he said, "Montana, do you know what an Ectopic Pregnancy is?"

"Um no…Oh my God did he just say pregnant? "Am I pregnant?"

"You were. You had what's called an Ectopic or tubular pregnancy. That is when the egg fertilizes outside the uterus and the fetus has nowhere to grow so it eventually bursts, which is what just happened to you. Your insides ruptured which is why there was so much blood."

Holy, this was really hard to digest.

"Does Ace know?"

"Not yet. I wanted to wait until you were awake before I called your brothers. I brought you to VGH instead of St. Paul's, they know my family here so they let me deal with this." Adam looked sad and his sadness make him look older. I realized that there was more he wasn't telling me.

"Adam, what else? Please don't keep me in the dark. What did the doctor say?"

He wouldn't look at me and he looked really upset, "Adam, whatever it is we can deal with this. Look at me and tell me the rest, please." He looked at me suddenly and in that very penetrating way of his. It was like he was seeing straight through to my soul.

"The doctors don't know if you can ever get pregnant again. You may never be able to have children. I'm sorry Montana. I feel like this is my fault."

"Your fault? That is ridiculous. How you can say that? It takes two, you know. I'm not Mary, this was not an immaculate conception and we have been very careful. It's a fluke, that's all. It's no one's fault."

"I should have been more careful."

"Adam, that is stupid. Don't even talk like that. We both know that you would never do anything like knock me up on purpose. Please don't feel that way. I don't blame you, it is simply something that happened. Please Adam, tell me you love me and hug me. I hate seeing you like this."

He leaned over me pulling me in close; we stayed like that until the doctor came in. The doctor explained how I would feel over the next few days and what to watch out for. He gave me the name of a gynecologist to see as a follow up in the next week or two.

We left the hospital and I was under instructions to take it easy for a few days. Just to lie down and drink plenty of liquids and eat iron rich foods until at least Wednesday. We went back to Adam's and I called Ace to let him know that I had the flu and I would be on the couch at Adam's for a couple of days. He said he would call school for me in the morning and would check on me later the next day.

I knew Danny was coming over in the morning to work on the art show with Adam so I decided to ask him for his advice on what to tell Ace. Adam and I were exhausted and only woke up when Danny came to the door in the morning.

"Hey dead beats, it's time to get up! We have lots to do today." Danny walked into the kitchen and made coffee and Adam helped me onto the couch so I could talk to Danny.

"You look terrible Mo, really pale. Are you sure it's just the flu?"

"Danny, before you and Adam start your day I have to talk to you." Adam stayed in the kitchen to make us breakfast. "There are a few things and this is really hard for me, so just bear with me okay?"

He nodded and looked at Adam who would not return his look. Dan frowned.

"What is going on? Adam, I have never seen you this down. Did someone die?"

Adam looked at Dan with a face like he was being slowly strangled. Unable to deal with his emotions he left the room and we heard his bedroom door close down the hall. Danny was about to follow him but I stopped him and told him to sit down.

"What has happened? What is wrong with Adam?" Danny asked, starting to sound panicked.

"Shhh, Danny. Adam had to take me into emergency last night. Something inside of me ruptured-- actually, a baby inside of me burst and I ruptured as a result. Adam is feeling like it is entirely his fault." Danny sucked in his breath and a range of emotions played on his handsome face.

This was so hard. *Why does life have to be so tough? Why is there so much pain?*

"I didn't know you were pregnant," he finally responded.

"Neither did I, or, we, I mean." A tear rolled down my cheek as I spoke.

"Jaimie kept trying to tell me something about you last night but she wouldn't come right out and say it. I guess she figured it out," he uttered softly, "and Adam is blaming himself?"

"Yes. I have tried to reassure him but he won't accept what I am saying. He won't even look me in the eyes Danny. The doctors told him they don't know if I can ever get pregnant again. I think that is what is bothering him the most."

"I'm so sorry, when will they know?"

"They won't. I have a follow up with a Gynecologist in a few weeks, maybe we will get some answers then. Dan, remember when I tried to commit suicide and you found me?" He nodded.

"I had images play like a slideshow in my mind. For the longest time I thought I was dead and then I realized these were pictures for me to see clearly, my life and what led to me trying to drown myself. Then…I saw dad. He was sent to convince me to live-- to tell me that there would be amazing things in store for me in my future."

"What did he tell you Mo?"

"That Adam and I would be married and that we *would have children*. That we would both become famous and wealthy. That my life would be amazing and all I had to do was choose to live. I never told anyone until today. I told Adam and he didn't even blink. The information had no impact on him as I had hoped. Now I feel like maybe my subconscious just conjured up dad to make me feel better. I didn't see only him. I'm at a loss as to what to do to make this right. And then there is Ace as well. I have thought about this and I don't think we should tell him yet. Alex needs him, worrying about me will distract him."

Silence followed my statement as we both sat lost in thought. What would be the right thing to do? Danny spoke first. "Let me talk to Adam, then we will decide what to do." He walked down the hall and entered Adam's bedroom, closing the door behind him.

I wanted to hear what Adam would have to say. I knew he would be completely honest with Dan as they were best friends and business partners. They couldn't afford secrets between them. So, I limped over to the bedroom where I could hear them.

"Adam, man. What is bothering you? Montana is fine. She is just tired and has a lot on her mind but she holds nothing against you. She loves you and your reaction is confusing her. So... tell me. What is going on?"

Adam was crying. Holy crap! I had never heard Adam cry. Danny just waited until he calmed down a bit. When he spoke his voice was clouded. He sounded broken. I wanted to burst in but I had to hear what he had to say.

"Dan, you need to take her home. I can't look at her right now. I'm so consumed with guilt. I know she doesn't blame me, she never would..."he finally continued, "but I blame me.... Please take her home."

I limped back to the couch and for the first time I questioned our relationship. Maybe it couldn't overcome everything, maybe dad never saw this coming and this was the end. These thoughts left me feeling empty. So, when Dan came back to say he was taking me home I didn't argue. I just allowed him to help me and we went home.

"It's not you, it's him now." Dan said on the car ride home. "Think about this. When you had stuff you couldn't deal with, what did you do?"

"I shut down. I was mentally unavailable," Dan smiled as I slowly came to my understanding, "until I was ready to deal with the loss and grieve...."

"Right. And the last time, how long were you gone for?" Now I was feeling deeply ashamed. I had so much to learn, poor Adam. I wouldn't even let him grieve.

"About seven months," I finally answered. "I'm an ass. I see what you're saying. You're such a good friend to him, Dan. You're a wonderful brother to me. Thank you." Suddenly I had a thought. "I'm worried about your show. It's coming up next week. With this interruption do you think you two will be ready?

"I'm not worried about it, Mo. I will keep Adam on track just as Alex and Ace will keep the band contract moving forward. All will be well, you'll see." Silent tears escaped and slid down my cheeks.

Dan parked and helped me into the house. Once he sat me on my bed, he stayed and held me. Then he got up.

"I have to get going, will you be okay here on your own?"

I nodded and asked, "Can you pass me the shoe box from under my bed, please? The one with mom's name on it."

He was just leaning under the bed when he poked his head back up, "Why do you need it?"

"I need to feel close to her, please pass me the box."

"You'd better not be messing with me Montana. If I come home and you have lost it I will phone Ace at work and tell him everything."

"I promise you I will be fine. She has some great stuff in her diary. You know, words of wisdom, that kind of stuff. You should read it sometime." He looked thoughtful at that.

"Maybe I will," he said absently and stood up. "Okay, I have to move it, and you're good?" I nodded.

"When Ace gets home, let him know that Adam was starting to feel like he was coming down with the flu too. So, I brought you home so he could rest."

"Okay," I responded. And with that he left.

I lay in bed and read mom's diary for two hours. Everything had happened to her. The stories were so much like my own, nothing about tubular pregnancy though. I guess I cornered the market on that one in the Stanford home. Reading her stuff made me feel better. I fell asleep and only woke up when I heard Alex come in and yell out, "Anyone home?"

"I'm here," I yelled out.

One look at me confirmed his thoughts, "What happened to you last night? I woke up in the middle of the night with a horrible stomach ache. I thought it was nerves and then realized it was probably you." I told Alex the entire story including the plan to not tell Ace until the contract was signed. He had a similar response to Danny, a slow exhalation like a balloon that is too full and needs to let out some air to relieve the pressure.

"When are the meetings with the agents for the record companies?" I asked, when we both fell silent.

"Tomorrow. Soon enough, don't you think?"

I smiled, "Yes. Are we all supposed to be there?"

"Only if you want to be included in the negotiations...." Alex looked at me doubtfully.

"Alex, you know what I want and need so you can do it for the both of us."

"Ace, Otter, the lawyer and I will hammer it all out."

"You found a lawyer?"

"Yeah Ace did. He called dad's lawyer and got a referral, so we're good there. Ace and I have written down what we want-- let me grab it. Maybe you can think of something to add." He went and got the list and read it to me.

"What do you think?" he asked.

"It sounds good to me. I do have one question, though. What is more advantageous for the band, a short or long contract? I mean, what if something better comes up and we're locked in? What does Otter think?"

"He thinks the same way I do. There are pros and cons to long and short contracts. With the long we have guaranteed income and exposure and a five album deal. With a shorter contract we can play the field but that is not necessarily a good thing. Bottom line is, if we feel our contract has been breached in any way we can break it. There could be an out for us if we get itchy feet. Eventually I may want my own studio and create my own label but for now this should work for us just fine."

He had thought of everything, he was becoming the star I always knew he could and would be. He will go all the way. As for me? I clung to the vision that Adam and I would be together, that we would have children, and I would be famous....

"Alex, are you sure you want me to be the drummer? If you prefer someone else it won't hurt my feelings or anything." He gave me a look that said don't be an idiot. "Don't feel obligated to me because I'm your sister is all I'm saying," I finished lamely.

"I want you. The band only works with you in it and Otter agrees with me. Hey, if something happens and one day one of us wants to quit or move on to something else? We will worry about it then. For right now, we are going to hit the big time together just like I always pictured."

An unseen burden had been lifted and I felt ready to take this on. I looked at Alex with my mischievous grin, "Well then let's kick some butt, and make some money, brother." He laughed and gave me a hug, "You're on!"

Alex went to make some tea and then we sat drinking our tea and dreaming of how we were going to spend our money.

We would begin in the studio right after school just like we did now. Then take the summer off because I'd be enjoying my Christmas present with Adam. In the fall we would get the album ready and take off on our first eight week European tour. We would be back for the record release of Dec 1st and have December off. Then back to the studio the first week of January the following year. That was the plan.

We were still chatting when Ace arrived home. "Hey, it's those famous Stanford twins," he said as he entered my room and joined us on the bed.

"How are you feeling, peanut?"

"Better thanks," I said and he gave me a kiss on the forehead.

"Rest up, we have meetings tomorrow." he said rubbing his hands in anticipation. I looked to Alex for help.

"Ace, Montana and I have gone over everything, she trusts us to negotiate her contract for her with whatever company we choose and she has given us power of attorney for tomorrow's meetings."

"Wonderful news little brother but I still think she should be there."

"But Ace, we are only meeting with the three different agents to listen to their spiel and then choose one so why does she need to be there?"

"They want all three of you to be there and meet and talk with you all before they lay out their proposal so she needs to be there." Alex was about to say something else but I shook my head no. If we pushed it now Ace would know something was up.

"It's no problem chief. I'll be there with bells on."

"That's my girl," he said.

He went into the kitchen to make dinner. Alex looked over to me, "Are you insane?" he whispered, "You won't make it."

"The less I move the better. The doc had some concern about me hemorrhaging. I will take it easy," I promised.

"I think we should tell him Mo."

"No. I'll be okay. If I start to feel really bad then I will go and lay down in the car after my turn with each of the agents." Danny came home as we were all sitting down to eat. "You're up," he said to me. "Feeling better?"

"A little," I answered. "How is Adam?"

"Okay, trying to recover...."

"Danny," Alex said redirecting Danny's attention from me to him, "we are all meeting with the agents tomorrow, Mo too." I shot Alex a dirty look but he just ignored me. Danny frowned.

"I don't think you should be doing that. You should be staying in bed, isn't that what the doc said to you and Adam?"

Ace asked. "What are you talking about little bro?"

"When I went over to Adam's this morning to work on the art show he suddenly came down with this weird flu virus that Mo has and the family doctor came by to check on them. He told both of them to stay in bed and let the flu run its course. That is why I brought her home. So, I think she should stay in bed and you guys just act proxy for her."

"That's what I said," Alex chimed in. Danny looked over at Alex and winked at him.

"But she looks fine," Ace said, "don't you guys think so?" They were shaking their heads no.

"I think it would be a mistake," Danny said and Alex nodded in agreement. Ace finally agreed and the topic was dropped. I think all three of us breathed a sigh of relief. Alex was doing the dinner dishes so I took the opportunity to talk to Danny in my room.

"What happened when you went back? What did Adam say, is he okay?" Danny sighed, "We worked. He didn't want to talk about what had happened, so our topic of discussion stayed on the art show."

"I get that, but how do you think he is Danny? Seriously, I need to know your thoughts. You're his best friend."

He sighed, "Not well. Adam takes everything to heart, like most artists do. Also, he takes responsibility for you one hundred percent so he feels like he doesn't deserve you because he let you down."

I thought about that, "Is there anything I can do? He's been there for me through...well, everything. How is it possible that I can't be there for him?"

Suddenly a horrific stabbing pain shot through me. Looking under the covers there was blood. If I didn't get back to the hospital I had been warned that I could bleed to death.

"Danny, you better take me to the hospital right now, to VGH where Adam took me last night. The doctor there knows my case and I should see him. I'm bleeding again. Tell Ace I have gone to bed and when the coast is clear I will sneak out the front and you can drive me."

"Montana, please let's tell him. I hate lying to him and if you have to stay he will find out anyway."

"No he won't. This is Adam's family doctor and they let me through with Adam's okay."

"Yes, but Adam won't be there. So, how is this going to work?"

"Let me worry about that part. You just get Ace distracted, get Alex to help and I'll handle the hospital thing."

Danny left and I phoned Liza. I needed to phone her anyway and tell her to help her son because I couldn't. She answered the home line and I spilled. I told her the summarized version because Danny was signaling to me that the coast was clear. She promised to let the doctor know I was coming, and she thanked me for telling her about Adam.

As I hung up the phone I hoped that I had done the right thing by putting my trust in Liza. I didn't have a healthy trust of women. The only one I had let in since my mom died was my friend Chrissie, and I had no sisters so my sense of female companionship had never been strong.

I snuck out the front door and Danny was in the car with the lights off. I crawled in and with clenched teeth asked him to hurry.

"Just hang in there, Mo!" Danny said flying through traffic over the Granville street Bridge. By the time we got there I was sluggish from blood loss. Danny carried me through the emergency doors, Dr. Sun was ready for us, and that's when I passed out.

I woke up a while later in a recovery room and saw Danny. "Yo bro, how long have I been out?"

"Not long, maybe two hours. They just brought you in here about half hour ago."

"Am I okay?"

"You will be. There was another baby Mo. Why it didn't miscarry with the first I don't know but maybe the doctor can shine some light on that."

I threw up in the bowl on the table beside me. Oh! How cruel fate could be. Twins! *Just like me and Alex* was all I could think and it made me so sad. I knew I was too young and I knew the timing was bad. I knew all those things, but to miscarry twins I felt the loss even though I hadn't known they had been there.

"Did the doc say when I could go home?" I asked quietly.

"You've lost a lot of blood in the last twenty four hours. They want you to stay till morning and then you can come home."

"Okay, you go home and cover for me in the morning. Don't let Ace go in my room. He and Alex have their first meeting at 9:00 so when they leave you can come and get me and take me home and then you can go and work with Adam on the show."

"Do you really want me to leave?" Of course I didn't. If I had said that he never would have left. Instead I said yes. He left with the promise to call and check on me later.

I was pondering the cruelties of life when Liza walked in. My eyes got big but I didn't say anything. She was probably there to rag on me for involving her perfect family in such a scandal.

"How are you feeling dear?" she asked.

"Terrible, actually. Did you see Danny on his way out?"

"Yes but he didn't see me. I gather from what you told me that no one knows you called me?"

I nodded, "Listen Liza, I am not here to cause problems. My main concern is Adam. He is reacting badly to all of this and I can't seem to help him. I overheard him talking to Danny and he said the sight of me was upsetting. I'm sorry the hospital dragged you down to verify me or whatever they do," I said, as silent tears slid down my face, 'but I will be fine, please go home and be with your family."

She looked me straight in the eyes and I returned her look tears and all. "You're certainly a tough little thing, and I am with my family." She said with a smile. "I will help Adam but I feel you are making a mistake in not telling him. Is there anything else I can do for you?"

I shook my head no and added that Danny was corning for me in the morning as only he and Alex knew about my situation.

"Just don't tell anyone and that is all I need. Thanks again for phoning Dr. Sun, he was ready for me when we arrived."

Danny arrived the next morning. After receiving some quick instructions from the doc he took me home. He set me up with food, water and tea and then headed over to Adam's. I lay there all day. Alex called at one point to see how I had made out. I didn't tell him about the second baby, the twin, as I felt it was too personal to share on the phone. Instead, I told him I was back to square one as far as the resting thing went so he would be celebrating our birthday tomorrow without me.

"How is it going on your end?" I asked, hoping for some good news.

"Awesome," he responded, with genuine enthusiasm. "We are getting everything we are asking for. I really like the guy from Atlantic Records, so I'm leaning that way. I've got to run. I'll talk to you later."

I tried calling Adam but there was no answer. I closed my eyes and must have fallen asleep. I woke to the sound of my own screaming and Danny shaking me wake. Devil eyes had been in my dreams taunting me and laughing at me. I was a sweaty mess.

v"How is he?" I croaked. Dan passed me a water glass.

"He seemed better today. Hey, how about some tea?" he asked, already heading to the kitchen.

"That would be great," I called out to his retreating form. I was happy to stay in bed. I had no energy despite my long nap.

Footsteps approached my door, "Is the tea ready?" I asked, as the door opened. Adam stood in my doorway with two steaming cups of green tea. I felt like I had really been through the wringer since last we talked but he looked it-- still gorgeous, but tired.

Neither of us said anything as he sat down on my bed and handed me my tea. Finally I broke the silence by asking, "What are you doing here? I thought the sight of me was too painful for you right now?"

He had a guilty look on his face, "Did Danny tell you that?"

"No Adam, he would never have done that, I snuck down the hall and listened in. I overheard your conversation with him."

He smiled a small smile, "I should have known," he said. "You are always in the know, aren't you Montana?" I didn't answer, instead I prudently sipped my tea until he went on.

"My mom came to my apartment last night for a nightcap." I choked on my tea and he took it from me and set it down. He gave me his penetrating look while I looked anywhere but directly in his eyes. I can't lie to Adam. He always knows.

I chirped, "Oh, that's nice. She is a lovely woman. How is she?"

"We had a very interesting discussion, one the like of which we never had reason to engage in before."

"Oh?"

"It was enlightening. She said her female intuition told her I needed a visit. As she completely lacks female intuition I figured it was 'someone' who enlightened her. Was it you?"

"Was it me, what?" I asked putting on my most innocent face.

"Let me spare you. She told me she visited you in the hospital, that you had to go back and that you had a second miscarriage."

"I asked her not to tell you anything. You need to focus on your show, not this. I can handle it on my own."

He leaned down till he was just inches from my face, "Twins."

I flinched and replied, "Yes, there were two and now there are none, and maybe never any."Tears leaked from the corners of my eyes.

"Montana, I'm sorry I've been such a putz. I told you before I have never lost anything that really meant anything to me... and seeing you like that scared me. And then, the loss of what might have been, I just became consumed with thoughts of what was lost instead of what I have."

"Your mother must have the worst opinion of me."

"On the contrary, she thinks you're an amazing young woman."

"Really, did she say that?"

He smiled, "Yes, and she also said that if I didn't get my butt over here pronto and find a way of making it up to you then I was a fool."

I sighed. "I sure like your mother," I said with a small laugh.

"Now, drink your green tea Miss Stanford. I hear it has healing properties."

"Oh, so you're a doctor now, are you?" I grinned. "Did you want to do a full exam, Dr. Northrop?"

He laughed and then sobered immediately. "My mom said the doctor told her you would have bled to death if you had taken much longer to get to the hospital. They had to top up your blood supply and still you haven't told Ace? Don't you think that's a mistake?"

"Nothing is harder than feeling the loss of what we might have had. The biggest mistake is you thinking you alone are to blame. You are the most important thing to me, Adam. Danny reminded me what a selfish twit I can be. I wanted you to have the space you needed to get over the loss and come back to me. I didn't want you to know about the second miscarriage. If I had my choice I wouldn't have shared the information with anyone. It is my body and a very personal loss to me, so no, I don't think not telling Ace is a mistake. My only question now is are we still we? Do you still want me, and am I still your muse?"

He sat back and assessed me so deeply I felt my soul was bared and I had no defenses....

"Yes. You're stuck with me Stanford."

Chapter 6

The group of merry contract negotiators walked through the front door about half an hour later. Alex and Otter plopped down on the bed and relayed the day. They were so excited they verbally tripped over each other in their retelling.

Ace popped his head through my bedroom door. "Are you still in bed? Get dressed, we are going out to celebrate."

I looked to Adam for support. He spoke up. "Ace, we will have to party at home tonight. Montana is not ready to get out of bed."

Ace looked confused, "What is going on? Aren't you the ones being overly dramatic for a change? It is just a little flu, she will be fine."

"Ace," Adam said bracing himself. "It is not the flu. You need to be quiet and listen to your sister. She has something important to tell you."

Ace looked offended but he sat down and shut up. I told him the whole story right from the night in Bino's to my second visit to the hospital the previous night. His eyes glazed over. He sat staring but not seeing.

"Ace, are you okay? Are you going to say something?" I ventured.

Ace had come a long way since dad died, but while I expected his wrath, if he lay the blame solely at Adam's door it could get ugly.

Ace surprised me. "Damn. You should have told me, but I understand why you didn't." He paused briefly. Then said, "You were going to come to the meetings today." He wasn't asking me, he was making a statement.

Adam looked to me for an explanation. I had omitted that part of the story in my retelling. The look on his face spoke volumes -- we would have a discussion later.

I answered Ace. "Yes. You said I needed to. Danny and Alex would have found a way to get me out of the meetings. I wasn't concerned about that."

"You told Danny and Alex before me?"

Ha, here was the crux of my brother. A control freak. The fact the mighty Ace didn't get to know first seemed more important than what had actually occurred. More than likely, he was probably hurt that he was the last to know. In that moment. I didn't care about how he felt. I was pissed off with the conversation.

"My body. My choice on how to deal with it. The band needed you more than I did. End of story."

"Adam, can you give us a minute? He nodded and walked out to the living room, closing the door behind him. Ace watched him leave and once again surprised me with his compassion.

"I know you're angry, that came out all wrong. What I meant to say is are you okay? I need to know how you're feeling about what has happened."

Those simple sentences broke down my defenses. In that moment I realized control freak Ace was himself being my guardian and protector.

"Old." That word seemed to summarize my feelings completely as I spoke it.

"You and me both, kid." Amazingly we laughed. He gave me a gentle hug and helped me to stand and move to the couch in the living room. We were done for the moment. I needed a drink. We toasted the guys and their negotiating finesse. In that heady moment, we relished our success and the long-term vision that had been planted inside of us.

I felt rich. Seventeen and rich. I grinned as I anticipated how this contract would bring me a new found independence.

Next up, I needed to be an asset for my family the night of Danny and Adam's gala. To show my full support I had to be at my best. I spent the next few days investing in my health. Adam's family chef had supplied me with iron rich foods for my blood. Antioxidant rich smoothies for my immune system. Rich, dark coconut-based curries for comfort. I dutifully consumed them and supplied myself with plenty of rest.

The morning of the art show I was feeling well enough to shop with Jaimie for a new outfit to wear. Jaimie knew exactly what to get because she had been to so many art openings and galas. I had the money to buy whatever I wanted. That was a liberating feeling. On the coattails of that liberation I realized that I should only purchase what I really needed and not waste money.

Having means wasn't about senseless choices. Then I rolled my eyes. *Really Montana? Go and be frivolous? When have you ever done that? Dur. Like never.* I laughed out loud. "What's so funny?" Jaimie asked.

"I just loved the look on that sales lady's face when we walked out without buying anything."

"I don't know why she was so upset. There were at least a couple of things we didn't try on." I snorted at Jaimie's little joke and wondered at her ease in this world. While we were looking through various stores I asked Jaimie how the pricing typically worked at art events and what to expect the price range to be at the guys' show.

"The cheapest piece is $3,000.00 and the most expensive will be around $15,000.00. This show has gotten tons of media attention. That's unusual for such a novice art event. The papers have tied the band's success with Danny's art launch. You're being called the entrepreneurial family and that's in addition to how connected Adam's family is in this town. Even people that aren't normally art enthusiasts will be in attendance because they are music fans. The cameras will be flashing all night and the society section of the paper tomorrow will be full of pictures of your family. How you look and how you act is critical to the guys' success."

We walked into Prada and there I found the perfect black suit that screamed rich, successful, and sexy. A fitted pencil skirt and suit jacket. I loved it! I also purchased a red camisole for under the jacket and new heels. Next on our list was the hair salon.

I couldn't remember the last time my hair had been cut. It fell in long wavy, curly layers. I had it re-shaped and a few inches taken off. Jaimie suggested streaks and I got those as well. On our way back home, I went to the bank and took out $10,000.00 in spending money. Then, I went home to rest for a few hours before leaving for the show.

I was almost asleep when I felt something under my pillow. I reached under and pulled out a little box with a note attached. *I realize I have been very busy and we have seen little of each other. Here is a gift I was hoping you would wear tonight, Love Adam.*

I opened the box and inside were diamond studs. They were big, like the ring. They must be one carrot. I smiled as I put them on and then fell into an exhausted asleep. When I awoke I could feel the excitement in the house. Alex and I were going together in a limo that Adam was sending over for us.

I called Adam before we left. "Adam, I just want you to know that tonight is going to be awesome, and if I forget to tell you later I want you to know I'm really proud of you."

I heard him chuckling. "What time are you getting here, brat?"

"The limo has just arrived so, no worries, I will be there to hold your hand." He chuckled again and we hung up. Alex came out of his room. We checked each other out.

"You look like a million bucks, sis."

I smiled. "*We* look like a million bucks."

"Well, you look like you're at least twenty years old."

"Really?" I said. "Do you think Adam will notice?"

"I can safely say if he doesn't then he is blind and stupid."

"You look like a rock god. Let's go stun some people and help the guys sell some art."

We arrived to a very busy red carpet. Limos pulled up and pulled out. The rich made a show of their wealth. Northrop connections, I mused. Liza would make sure her connections showed support for her son.

There were dozens of photographers and so many flashes that I nearly stumbled. Alex and I were recognized and stopped for pictures and questions. He kept me steady with his arm linked through mine. He took the lead and answered questions, while I smiled and nodded.

Once inside, I was blown away by the amount of people and art that crowded the gallery. Suddenly, I felt awkward. Everywhere I looked I saw me. My face was on every wall. Adam's muse. It felt like my whole life was on those walls. Adam had captured my most vulnerable moments. It was personal and I didn't know how to react.

Alex felt my struggle. He still had a hold on my arm and pulled me closer to whisper.

"You must have known what it would be like. This is a blown up, better version of Adam's bedroom. You are his art."

"I guess I never thought about it. Kind of funny that money will be made off my face."

Alex laughed and moved away releasing my arm. "Yeah, no kidding. Most likely anything bought tonight with us in it will rise in value as our careers do." Apparently, we were not the only ones who had that thought. Even as the words left Alex's lips we heard others saying they were there for the deal of the century.

I caught sight of Adam talking to some wealthy somebodies. Abruptly, he looked up and glanced around. Looking for me no doubt. I saw his eyes roam over me and then snap back. He did a double take. Ha. He had not recognized me. The outfit and new hair had done their job. I got him. I watched him excuse himself and walk over to join Alex and me.

"This is incredible!" I gushed as he shook Alex's hand. "I'm so excited for you!" I gushed again.

"I'll tell you what's exciting. I'm going out with the most beautiful creature I have ever seen. You are truly a vision." I blushed and Alex left.

"I didn't expect to see my whole life on these walls." I said changing the subject.

"Don't be so vain. It's not all you. I think I could find one or two pieces tucked away that have absolutely nothing to do with you."

We laughed. "I have to mingle. Take a look and pick a piece for yourself. You get first choice as a gift from me."

"Oh no. No more gifts, I'm here to invest." I was about to walk on when I spotted Adam's parents arriving. I waited to greet them.

"I don't know what's bigger, your band or this show!" Geoff said with a smile as he drew me in for a warm hug.

"I was about to start the tour, would you two like to join me?"

"Love to kiddo, but I see Ace and Kristine have just arrived."

He was gone leaving Liza with me. "You look radiant, my dear. How are you feeling?" She embraced me and her warmth radiated through me.

"I think I am on the mend. Thanks again for all your help." We walked and periodically we would stop for photos or for me to sit down and rest. I stopped to examine a group of sculptures that I had not yet seen.

The first sculpture was called '*Sorrow*'. A bust of my head with my eyes closed and abstract breaks in the surface made it almost unrecognizable. It was me after I had been beaten by Mercy and her gang before Adam and I started going around. I had no idea he had connected so deeply with me even though he'd mentioned that when we first met for real. I lingered while Liza moved on.

I caught up with her at the last statue. It was of two babies intertwined. Twin babies. I staggered and would have lost my balance if Liza had not been there. She steered me over to a nearby divan. Conveniently, a waiter came by with a tray of drinks and Liza grabbed me a whiskey.

I gave her a questioning look. "Whiskey is a fine remedy for restoring the nerves." She said. I smiled and shot it back.

"Liza, the statue-- it looks like Alex and me but I know it isn't. I guess Adam found a way to grieve." She smiled. A single tear ran down my cheek. I felt ready to go and examine it. Liza helped me up and walked me over as she murmured how lovely it was. This was the one. The piece I wanted. I was still staring, mesmerized by it when Adam came up from behind.

I could hear camera flashes all around us. I felt like I was drifting and couldn't move my focus from the statue to Adam or anything else in the room. "Are you okay?" He asked gently.

"Yes...No...I don't know. I have never seen anything like it. That is the one I want to buy."

Adam hugged me from behind and smelled my hair. "I had Jaimie put it on reserve for you. Come my lovely. Let's go find her and get your statue."

Adam led me to Jaimie and Dan and went off to mingle. Danny whistled. "You have never looked so grown up."

"Very funny. Don't blow my cover."

I was about to head over to the payment station with Jaime when we were approached by some art dealers. Dan made the introductions and after a seemingly interminable discussion I grabbed Jaime and bee-lined for the reserve table. She seemed a bit irritated and said, "Gee, you must love this." From her tone, I could tell it wasn't a compliment.

I paid for the sculpture. The cost was $4,000.00 and worth every penny. I decided that I needed to purchase a piece of Dan's work. After examining a series, I found a painting that he had done of dad. It was abstract but I knew who it was. He was in the ocean with a dolphin. I remembered the story he told about that dolphin from the last time he had visited.

It hadn't been sold yet so I went back to the table and bought it. Enough walking. I was feeling weak and needed a seat. I grabbed some champagne and sat. I watched the activity around me. I saw Alex with a crowd of young women around him. I could see Ace with a group of men and women. Geoff and Liza were among them. I smiled. Ace and Alex looked happy. They were comfortable in their element.

I watched Adam speak with his mother briefly. Then he joined me. "How are you feeling? You look a little pale."

"I'm okay. A little hungry. I just needed a rest...and this." I held up my champagne glass. "How long do we have to stay?"

"Most of the show has sold... so an hour? How does that sound?"

"Are you tired Adam?"

"Yes. The endorphins are starting to taper off and I'm relaxing. All I want to do is celebrate in private with my family, my girl, have a few drinks and maybe sleep for a week. Unfortunately, I have a little more butt kissing to do." He grinned.

An hour later the highly successful Stanford and Northrop families took a limo to a fancy supper club that Ace had booked in anticipation of a successful night. An hour sitting and drinking champagne had done me a world of good. I let the past week go and relaxed. Our festive group was in a fine mood. Adam and Dan gave themselves permission to let go and celebrate their success. There was much toasting and merriment. Everyone was slightly drunk, or in Adam and Dan's case a little hammered.

When the limo dropped us off. I needed Ace's help getting Adam in the house. I laughed as an inebriated Ace and a thoroughly drunken Adam staggered slowly up the few stairs to our front porch. They collapsed on the porch swing which in turn collapsed on the deck.

A roar of laughter erupted from the two of them. Alex seemed a little more on the ball and stood beside me grinning. "I say leave them there."

"Well, I would love to but it is still cold out so help me get them up."

"No, that would put a lot of strain on your body. I can handle this." The next half an hour will be forever imprinted on my mind. As Ace, Alex and Adam all struggled to collect themselves and get into the house I almost peed myself from laughter and a surplus of alcohol. The brat in me couldn't resist a whole lot of picture taking. If I ever made the collection public I would call it the *Debacle of the three A's*.

In the morning Adam and I headed for the ferry. Despite his desire to be in bed for a week we had booked a hotel on Vancouver Island for some much-needed privacy and quality time. While I waited in the car, Adam grabbed the morning paper from the stand hoping for some shots of last night's show. A picture of Adam and Danny was featured on the front cover of the arts and entertainment section of the Province Newspaper. **'LOCAL BOYS MAKE IT BIG'**. Two entire pages were dedicated to the show.

There was my face again, not just in Adam's art but in photo after photo. Ugh. There I was with Geoff, Liza and Ace, then Adam with his arms around me. Then, a whole wack of shots with high profile guests. Included in the follow up article **'STANFORDS IN THE MIX'** was the recent contract signing of the band with Atlantic Records...Otter, Alex, and me again, of course. Then there was a write up on Geoff and his companies with a mention of Ace, his boy wonder, but finally not his sister, thank Christ.

The article gave Adam and Danny's work rave reviews. A relief for both men I was sure. Sometimes the critics could be fickle. The success of sales had nothing to do with what they thought of you. Once aboard the ferry we received many looks. Almost everyone was reading the Province paper.

We decided to grab more coffee and take it below deck to Adam's car and hide until it was time to drive off.

We laughed as we drank our coffee. "This is a big game changer. Literally within two weeks of each other our stars have risen."

I had been doing well with the stresses of the past few weeks. Miscarriages, calling on Liza, dealing with contracts and still having to find time to do homework in preparation for final exams. We all kept the hammer down(pedal to the metal, nose to grindstone, whatever you want to call it), and did what was needed. Last night had been a taste of the type of events Adam and I and my entire family would be part of in future.

That had my head spinning a bit. I needed to ground. I needed some normalcy or something. I didn't know what I needed only that I needed something from him.

"Montana, are you okay, are you having second thoughts?"

I looked down to my lap, my hands were gripping each other, I hadn't even noticed until I saw them. Tears blurred my eyes. "No, I just feel, um, like life has suddenly gotten way bigger than I pictured. Events like last night will happen frequently in the future and not just for you and Dan but for me and Alex as well. I think he has always wanted that. He is built for it. You are built for it. Dan and I ...well, we are just along for the ride. At least that is how it feels at the moment.... I guess what I want to know, will it ever be okay for me to just be me and to just be with you? Or will I always be beholden to this big picture?"

I stopped talking. I didn't know what I was saying, I just needed someone to understand how I felt. Adam drew me onto his lap in the car and hugged me for a long time. I felt the tension drain from my body. I hadn't realized I was so wound up.

"I will take care of you, never fear. If you start to fall I will pick you up. If your career begins to consume you I will fix it. If you want to be home, you will be home. If you want to be the biggest star in the world I will be your biggest fan. You are not alone. I hear you."

I nuzzled in close. He had said what I needed to hear. No matter what was happening in our worlds, he and I would be the one constant. We would decide our fate and take control of how we wanted to live.

After spending a full twenty-four hours in our room we decided to venture out and see the beautiful city of Victoria. After a stroll around the harbor we went shopping. We were noticed. People pointed and whispered behind their hands but no one approached us.

We checked out a local gallery whose owner had come to the opening at Liza's invitation. Adam talked with him while I looked at some of the work. Near the back he had photos of various artists. One was of Adam's mom. I brought Adam over to show him and the owner followed us. "We are old friends. I knew her as a young photojournalist back in the day. It was lovely to see her at your opening. I guess talent runs in the family," he said with a smile. I requested a copy of the photo before we left. I had an idea for a Christmas gift for Liza.

Back at the hotel, we relaxed in a big jacuzzi tub for two. I felt amazing. I had needed de-stressing. As I soaked I reflected on the past few weeks. We were headed home tomorrow and I would be in the thick of things. I found it hard to keep perspective when my life was loud. Here in this tub my life was quiet. A good time to see things clearly.

As I dried off I shared some of my thoughts with Adam.

"I feel like a fake, like I'm riding on Alex's coattails. He is the one who made this happen and he is the only one who really deserves the success."

"Hang on a minute. Just because you never saw yourself getting this far does not mean you didn't earn it. Think about it. You were the band's first writer. For two years you wrote all the songs and gave them to Alex. Do you think he would have gone that far without you? You picked up the drums when he needed you the most and you trained him a new drummer when you couldn't play. If you're basing your opinion on consistency he's got you beat hands down. He has stuck it out and made his dream a reality, but he didn't do it alone. Never forget that."

I chewed on that for a moment. Adam was right. Timing had been very strategic in our combined success. Where would Alex be without me? A good question and one to contemplate further. The next day we checked out and went home.

Chapter 7

Europe was amazing! Adam showed me all I wanted to see and more. I had dreamed as a child of seeing the tower of London and had hoped to see the ghost of Ann Boleyn. I didn't her ghost but I felt them in those tiny cells were people had been kept. The lower the prisoner's station the lower and damper the cell. Just seeing them made me feel claustrophobic. And although I did not see a ghost or any other specter I did feel tremendous sorrow. Like the structure itself groaned under the weight of sadness.

Other highlights included Hadrian's Wall in Scotland. Another childhood dream. I imagined what it must have been like for those early Roman soldiers defending one part of Britain from another. We rented mopeds and drove the road along the wall. Not as monumental as the Great Wall of China I was sure but the wall spoke to me of civilizations come and gone. I had really enjoyed Scotland and knew I would go back in the future and explore more of its gems.

On the flight home I reviewed the sites and luxuriated in the feeling of having 'gone to Europe'. Every kid I knew when asked what they planned on doing after high school said they were going to Europe. It was a rite of passage and I had feared I would not make mine. I did and it was amazing, even more than my imagination could have conjured. I saw now why people always said they never have enough time because there was so much to see. I knew I would return.

Danny was at the airport to pick us up. He seemed like he had a lingering cold as he shared with Adam all the wonderful things that had been happening for his career in our absence. I had thought a lot about Dan while I was away. The night of the art opening Dan was the only one who had not seemed in his element. Now he seemed unnaturally agitated and I wondered what else had happened while we had been away. Money, money, money.

Adam had made a lot of money through gallery sales. I had made money also as another installment had been deposited into my account. The concept that money could come in while you were away was a foreign one. I knew I was really lucky to have this in my life but when I heard nothing but numbers in the front seat conversation going on between Adam and Dan I turned my attention out the window, rolling my eyes.

I heard 'prints for mass production of posters and cards'. I had a moment of panic as I imagined someone buying my face as a greeting card. "Which ones are being mass produced?"

"What difference does it make?" Danny responded, glancing at me in the rear-view mirror. Reining in my panic for a moment, I watched Dan closely as I responded.

"A huge difference to me! Because Danny, a lot of those paintings are of me and I was never asked if I wanted my picture being mass produced to hang in offices or whatever they plan on doing with them."

Danny laughed. "Really? So what do you think is going to happen when they add in an entire profile of you and Alex in Rolling Stone or any magazine and people cut out those pictures and put them on their wall just like you did with *The Who*?"

We had just pulled up in front of the house and I opened the car door and threw up. Adam spoke up in my defence.

"She's just feeling a little insecure about being a success. It's a lot to take in and not just the band's but ours as well Dan. Just give her some time, she'll be fine."

I sat back up and closed the car door. Dan's look wasn't compassionate at all when he said. "You and Alex have three days to practice before you start recording in the studio. I know he has some new stuff he wants you to hear."

"Seriously Dan, my brain still hasn't landed in Canada."

When I put myself together and came up I went into the house and Danny and Adam were still at it. Ace entered the room and I barely noticed as I was fascinated watching my quiet brother Dan talk non-stop. I finally noticed Ace and gave him a big hug. I wouldn't let go and he whispered "What's up?" in my ear.

"I'm scared," I whispered.

"Of what?" he whispered back.

"The future. It is looking mighty big."

He chuckled. "Don't worry, "I won't let you get lost." Alex came in from the garage and a big grin lit up his face. I leapt on him and we shared a big sibling hug.

"You look great," he said, "tanned and relaxed. I hope you rested up because the next five or six weeks are going to be intense."

Ace and Alex sat down and I began to talk about Europe. Following my lead, Adam moved the conversation from business to pleasure. Adam and I took turns for the next hour talking about our trip and the things we saw.

"Hey whose night to cook dinner?" I asked, as we wound down our tag team retell, "I'm starving."

"Cook? We don't cook anymore," Alex said.

"And why not?" I asked.

"Because we don't need to. We don't clean anymore either. We have a house cleaner instead."

I looked at Adam and then at Ace. "What is going on around here? What has happened to you guys? You're all acting pathetic! Someone drive me to the store. I'm shopping and this family is getting back on track as of right now."

Ace clapped his hands, "Good! Now it's two against two and I can't be out voted anymore." Danny drove Adam home and Ace and I went shopping.

"Has it been like this since I left?" I asked.

"Pretty much," he answered, "but to be fair, Danny is super busy right now and we don't know when he is going to be home. So, he eats wherever and whenever he can. I'm busy with my new job as everything I'm doing is project based, so my hours are all over the place. The only one who has been around regularly is Alex."

It made sense to me. "I never thought about how busy and separate our lives would become and what that would do to our lifestyle. The cleaning lady makes sense but we should have the fridge stocked and I think we should make the effort to eat at least one or two nights together. What do you think?"

"I agree," he responded. We took the groceries home and I made dinner that night. Afterwards, I made Alex do the dishes. He tried to argue that the maid would be there in the morning and I said, "That is no excuse for being a pig."

The next morning I was up first and made coffee. I heard Ace in the shower so I got his ready and left it on the bathroom counter for him. "Thanks peanut!" he yelled, "Glad you're back!" Danny had rented a small studio space where he could work and he was up and out the door next.

I woke Alex up when the maid arrived and we ate breakfast together. Otter walked in and I barely recognized him. He had grown about three inches that summer so he was finally over six feet. He had totally changed his image and he looked great.

I asked him to join us for breakfast and he sat down while I got more food. We discussed what we needed to focus on for the day; the studio had approved eight out of the twelve songs so far for recording. Those were the ones we were going to practice first.

I spoke with the maid on my way out to the garage and let her know things I felt needed to be done, including an overhaul on the place. "The works," I said, "and don't worry about the price on this one. I'll pay you separately."

She smiled and went to town on the house while I joined the guys in the garage. We worked for about three hours and it felt good to be back in the saddle, or on the stool in this case. We took a lunch break and then went back for two more hours and called it a day.

"God, that felt good." I said, "How do you guys feel?"

"You felt off to me," Alex said. Otter and I shared a look, but neither of us said a word.

"Come early tomorrow, Otter, and have breakfast with us again," I said as he was leaving.

"That would be great," he said as he left. Alex was in the kitchen grabbing a bottle of water and the maid, Doreen, was just leaving. I thanked her for her work. The place looked great and I gave her $100.00. "How about every Monday, Wednesday and Friday? Doreen, would that work for you?" She nodded, "How much are they paying you?"

"$8.00 per hour," she said, so I raised it to twelve and she thanked me and left.

I went into the kitchen and confronted Alex. "What is going on? I asked, "You're being a jerk. You need to chill out, and for your information I wasn't off, but your attitude is."

"Montana," he sighed, as he sat down and put his head in his hands, "I don't know what's going on and you're right. I am being a jerk and I don't know why."

I walked behind him and rubbed his back. He was really tense. When I felt him breathe and totally relax I stopped rubbing and sat down opposite him.

"Alex, you have just gone from being a local boy to super stardom and you feel pressure.What has happened is huge! I understand that it is your dream. Just relax. They liked us when we were just us, you don't need to be someone else."

He looked up and smiled, "You're right. I promise tomorrow will be better."

"Good," I said as I answered the phone. It was Adam.

"Hey brat, I miss you. What are you doing?"

"We just finished up and I was about to start dinner. Where are you?"

"Just leaving the studio and thought 1 would come over and join you. Dan has a date with Jaimie so he won't be coming home for dinner."

"Sounds great, see you soon," I said and hung up the phone.

"Was that Adam?"

"Yes."

"Is he coming for dinner?"

"Yes."

"What about Danny?"

"No. He has a date, apparently."

"How long has he been like this, Alex? He has never been distant."

"Oh that." he grinned, "Since the day you and Adam left, pretty much." Was it the success or was there something else going on? I went into the kitchen and started dinner. I was just finishing up when Ace and Adam walked through the door.

"Where is Dan?" Ace asked, as he came in and washed his hands.

"Out," I said, "he told Adam he had a date with Jaimie."

Ace frowned, "I told him I wanted him to be here tonight and he said he would." I shrugged and the four of us sat down and had a great dinner together. Alex left soon after to meet some buddies and Ace went to go and read some proposals he was making for work the next day. That left Adam and I alone.

He talked about the interviews he and Danny had that day. I listened while I cleaned up. Apparently, I was the only one concerned with keeping the place maintained. We snuggled on the couch afterwards and I asked Adam what he thought about going to Victoria for a few days again. He sighed, "I would love to Mo, but like Ace said, our schedules are at odds right now. It would be hard to figure out a time."

"I was thinking at Christmas, maybe we could all go over to Victoria and rent one of those penthouse suites for a few days, just play and have fun."

"That sounds really good," he said sleepily. His eyes were closed and I watched him. He was so beautiful.

"Adam?"

"Hmm," he intelligently replied.

"Come to bed, you're exhausted. Come and sleep with me, don't bother going home." I pulled his zombie-like form up from the couch, walked him to my room and pushed him onto the bed, took off his shoes, and covered him up.

I was feeling unsettled. There was something about Danny that concerned me and I couldn't put my finger on it. I wanted to speak with Ace so I knocked on his door, "Can I come in?"

"Sure. Come on in," he responded. I went in and sat down on his bed. "What's up?"

"Well, I'm concerned about Danny."

"Why, because he didn't show up for dinner?" Ace said with a chuckle. My face reddened.

"Ace. I'm serious. It has nothing to do with dinner, it' s his attitude. I mean, when he picked us up from the airport he was all business and money, which is fine, but he is never rude to me and he was a real jerk on the way home. He has lost weight and he looks pale. He's usually tanned at this time of

267

year, and I'm wondering what is up with him? Also, when I talk to him he won't look me in the eyes like he is trying to hide something from me, and that is just plain not him. Do you know who he is spending his time with other than Jaimie?"

He looked thoughtful for a minute. "The thing is, Montana, as Dan is an adult there is not much I can do. He doesn't want to talk to me and I can't put a leash on him. There is really nothing I can do."

"Oh really?" I said folding my arms. "Is that what you would say if it was me?"

He smiled, "No, if it was you I would be calling in the cavalry."

"Very funny," I said, and threw a pillow at him. "Honestly, if it was me how would you feel? What would you do?"

"It's different with you Montana. You have a knack for getting into trouble, more than anyone I know. So, if it was you, I would investigate right away, hopefully before you screwed up. But you and I both know that hasn't always worked. You're sneaky. When you want something or think you're right, no one seems to be able to stand in your way and that's a great quality to have. When you make the right decision, which you are doing more and more as you grow up, you do amazing things. It is also your greatest weakness because you can be reckless and selfish also, but Dan has rarely ever gotten in trouble. He's easygoing and even when he was little he rarely ever got into trouble."

This was turning out to be an interesting conversation. "What about Alex, what if it was him?"

He laughed, "Really? The only trouble Alex has been in is whatever he got caught doing with you. Mom used to think it was Alex instigating everything until one day she overheard you talking him into sneaking off to the school to play. It was then she realized that you were the ring leader. I had tried to tell her before, because I caught you all the time getting into mischief, but she didn't believe me until she caught you herself."

"Come on Ace," I said, rolling my eyes. "I couldn't have been that bad?"

"Do you remember painting the living room furniture with lipstick?"

"I never did that. That's horrible."

He laughed at me, "Remind me to tell you one day all the crazy stuff you have done."

I thought for a minute. "Okay, so he doesn't have a history of getting in trouble but something still isn't right. Just keep your eye on him when he is around. Watch him and see for yourself."

"Sure," he said. "Did Adam go home already?"

"No poor boy, he was exhausted so he is sleeping in my bed."

"Well it's no wonder, look at who he spends his time with," Ace said with a laugh. I tossed another pillow at him and walked out the door. I could still hear him chuckling as I walked to my room.

Montana, you can't save your brother. I have brought him to hell and I will keep him here with mommy. I will get them all, everyone you care about, everyone you love. Then I will get all the girls like you and you will see them all die. Then, when there is no one left to save you…. The red eyes laughed while they spoke.

I woke up screaming and Adam sat up like he had been struck by lightning. I hadn't had a nightmare the entire time we had been away. My second night home and red eyes was back. I told Adam what it said. He held me for a long time in silence and I thought he had fallen back to sleep. "Maybe it is time to see that doctor you had sessions with after you attempted suicide."

I didn't really think a doctor could help me this time. I felt this was a premonition, not my subconscious. It was a warning something dire was coming my way. I drifted off to sleep without answering.

The next morning, I rose early and made coffee and breakfast for everyone. I served Adam his in bed, we discussed Danny while he was eating. "Haven't you noticed a change in him?" I asked. "He is grumpy, mean, and doesn't make eye contact."

Adam was thinking while he was chewing. "I noticed, but I think it is stress. Clearly you do not?"

"No Adam. I don't think it is stress. That may be the reason why, but I think he is doing drugs."

"What?" Adam said sitting up, breakfast forgotten. "Why do you think that?"

"Because I know my brother. This is Danny we're talking about. I dismissed the thought when I first had it. But I have this gut feeling and you know those are never wrong. Ace won't take me seriously so I need your help."

I could see Adam's wheels turning. "I've read about this. If you're right, we have to watch for sudden disappearances for 20 min. or half an hour. Too short to do anything of consequence for business and too long to be something as small as just a bathroom break. I'll watch, but that is it. This could affect my partnership in a very negative way, but you may be right and that could be worse."

Otter arrived so I fed him breakfast and then we headed to the garage. After rehearsal, I called Jaimie and told her I would like to come down and have coffee with her privately. I hoped she would understand by my use of privately that I didn't want Dan to know. I headed down to the museum and we had coffee across the street in a bistro called Bananas.

"Jaimie, I need to ask you some questions about my brother."

"Really?" she said, "what do you want to know?"

"You guys are dating and you are helping him with his business so I thought you would know if Dan is doing drugs."

She looked at me. Her expression was blank but her body language was anxious. "Why would you think that?" she asked, making no eye contact as she did so. "I don't think so, Montana. I think I would know."

She lied as badly as me. I took a closer look at her. She was also pale and thinner. I played it cool. "Well I'm glad you cleared that up. Whew, I was concerned. But, as you say, you spend more time with him than anyone so if you don't think so then you must be right."

We parted company and I detoured to the studio so I could share my findings with Adam. Danny was there on the phone, having a heated discussion with someone. Adam kissed me. "Hi," he said surprised, "you're early."

"I know. I wanted to see you guys." I rolled my eyes In Danny's general direction.

Danny hung up the phone, "Hey Dan the man, how are you?" I asked.

His voice dripped ice as he said, "Do you have something to tell me?"

I acted confused, "Um, I don't think so?"

"Well think harder," he said, as he moved closer to me. His energy was all wrong. I felt threatened and automatically backed towards Adam.

"Dan, is there a problem?" Adam asked.

"Just stay out of it," he answered. "Now tell me what naughty things you did today, Montana." He knew about my meeting with Jaimie for coffee. That was probably Jaimie he had been talking to when I walked in.

I could play his game. I wasn't giving in so I put on my tough act. "What's it to you, Dan? Last time I checked you did whatever the hell you wanted. I'm just following your awesome example."

The ice in my voice matched his. His jaw was twitching. That was the sign that he was really pissed but we were already in this thing so I pushed harder. "If by naughty you mean did I have coffee with Jaimie? Hell ya, and she confessed that the two of you are doing drugs."

"You liar!" Watching him was fascinating. In that moment I saw such a huge array of emotions cross his face: Shock, shame, and anger. Rage actually, as I found out a moment later when he grabbed my arm, swung me around and slapped me for all he was worth. He grabbed my hair and pushed me down onto my knees.

Adam was in total shock, momentarily rooted. Recovering, he grabbed Dan. "What the hell are you doing, Dan? Get your hands off your sister."

Danny released me and was staring at me like he had just woken up out of a dream. Again many emotions played across his face: guilt, anger, hurt, but fear was the last one I saw.

As I got to my feet I proclaimed, "You can deny it all you want, Dan, but you are definitely screwing around with something." Dan was frozen, not yet ready to admit anything. "I love you enough to try and stop you, so if you don't want me finding anything out then I suggest you come clean. I will find out, even if I have to hire a detective, you think on that!"

I walked out on shaking legs and slammed the door behind me. I heard the door open and close. It was Adam. "Are you okay?" he asked.

"I'm fine. Listen, we are getting in your car and pulling out so we look like we are leaving and then we are going to stake him out."

"Okay...."

"When I met with Jaimie today I asked her if Danny was using drugs. She said no but I could tell she was lying. I'm sure they're both into the hard stuff."

"If you're right...."

"Jaimie and maybe a dealer will be walking through that door any minute."

"You goaded him on purpose, didn't you?"

"Yep," I smiled, "That is the West End way. I needed him to lose it and now he will be looking for a fix."

"You're pretty amazing. How do you know?" he asked.

"Call it intuition. That, and my old pal Matt dealt," I replied. "I may not have read up on it, but I've seen a thing or two."

Not long after, a car pulled up and Jaimie and two other guys got out. They headed up to the studio. Adam and I waited until they were inside and then snuck up the back stairs to listen. We heard Jaimie say, "She knows, Dan."

Adam and I looked at each other.

Danny spoke next. "I don't care what she thinks. She is just a little girl butting in where she shouldn't be. She has no proof so Adam and Ace won't believe her anyway. It's my life. I can do whatever the hell I want."

It went quiet, and then we heard heavy sniffing. I had heard enough and motioned Adam to follow me back downstairs. We got in his car and raced for my house. Now Adam had no doubt.

"Wow, you were right. He is into some bad stuff. Time to tell Ace." I nodded in agreement.

We found Ace was just sitting down to dinner.

"Hey, I didn't think you were going to be home tonight-- What the hell happened to your face?" Adam told him the story while Ace got me a bag of frozen peas to help bring down the color and the swelling.

I cut Adam off. "I think we should get Eddy and go over there and get Danny and put him in detox, what do you think?" Ace thought for a few minutes, digesting everything and thinking of options. Finally, he said, "I can't believe he had that reaction when you confronted him. He must be out of his mind."

"Ace," Adam spoke, "I've never seen him like that before. Whatever cover he had she blew which is why he was so angry. You can't reason with him, he's lost."

"Please Ace," I added. "Let's go and get him."

"Okay," he finally conceded. "Go call Eddy and we will go and get him." Alex happened to pick that moment to arrive home. He knew something was up.

"What is going on?" Adam gave him the run down while I phoned Eddy.

Ace had changed into his black jeans and black t-shirt, I did the same and so did Alex.

"What's with the black clothing?" Adam asked.

"These are our rumble colors. When something is about to go down, in case there is confusion, we all wear the same color. It also lets the other side know we are there for a fight and we won't leave until it is resolved, although I must say I never thought we would ever have to wear them for family."

Adam and I drove back to the studio in his car. Alex, Ace, and Eddy went in Alex's car. When we arrived, Jaimie's car was still parked. We crept upstairs and listened to them still snorting. Oh man, I felt so bad for Danny. I was struggling with the reality of his situation. Adam had the key so he unlocked the door and we spilled into the room.

All four of them looked up, startled. Danny wiped his nose and furtively glanced from one face to another and finally rested on mine. He gave me a look of pure hate as he laughed unnaturally. I felt my heart and legs tremble. *He hates me and I love him so much.* Adam squeezed my hand, he had seen the look too.

Ace was speaking; "Dan I want you to tell your friends to leave now. We would like to talk to you in private."

Danny was caught, no doubt about it. His dealer stood up, "Hey, we aren't leaving. We're just having a little party."

"The party is over," Ace said. "Now get out or I'm going to make you get out."

The dealer and his buddy checked out Eddy and Ace and determined that they didn't think they could take them, so instead he said, "Do you know who I am?"

"Yeah, I do," said Eddy, "and if you don't want to get arrested I suggest you leave now."

"Jaimie," Ace said, "you will go to your office and get every single contract and every piece of work you have for Adam and Dan and give it to Adam. He will go with you and make

sure you get it all. You're fired." She snapped up to her feet, obviously coked up as she tried to maintain her composure but succeeded in just looking twitchy and weird.

"Don't be ridiculous. You can't fire me, I have a contract with them. Right Danny?" That was clearly news to everyone but Danny. He was scratching his head, and couldn't help licking his finger and wiping the remains of a line off the table and rubbing it on his gums. His colour was terrible.

Ace concluded, "Your contract just expired, don't try to fight it." She bottled her reaction and nearly burst. She grabbed her stuff and she and Adam walked out.

"Dan, I know you're angry but this has to stop now."

"Screw you Ace," he finally said. "I can make my own decisions. I'm an adult, remember? And tell that little bitch," he pointed at me as his emotions stormed, "that I don't ever want to see her again, EVER!"

Ace remained the model of control. "Never mind Montana right now, she just loves you and wants to help you. Now listen Dan, we are taking you to detox and I know when your old self is restored you'll see how destructive this all is and be glad you are clean. So, are we dragging you out or will you come of your own free will?"

Danny stood up and walked over to pass us on his way to the door. At the last moment, he turned to me and spat right into my face. "I hate you." Then he, Eddy, and Ace walked out the door. I wiped the spray off and Alex and I watched from the window as the three of them got into Adam's car. Alex and I disposed of the evidence, locked up, then got into his corvette and headed home.

"I think I need a drink," I said. Alex agreed and we stopped to get some rum and some beer. We were not home long when Adam showed up with a box of everything from Jaimie's office. We had drinks and looked through and sorted the box. As none of us had eaten yet we ordered pizza and that's when Ace and Eddy showed up.

"Montana, it is worse than you thought. He did a lot of coke tonight. He might have overdosed if we hadn't got there when we did. I hope you know Dan doesn't hate you, that was the drugs talking." I nodded.

"Listen. Tomorrow night we, the three of us, need to go in and have an interview with the doctor. He needs to go over with us what to expect with the detox and recovery. He will be there at least one week and maybe a month. Adam, I'm afraid you're on your own for a bit with the business." Adam nodded.

"Montana, I know you and Alex start recording tomorrow, so I will meet you at the hospital at 7:00pm for our meeting with the doctor." Everyone accepted the grim reality we were all facing and seemed to hold our breath for a moment and then let it out.

Okay?" We said in unison. "Okay." Adam decided to go home with the box and finish sorting and figuring out what he had to do next. I thanked him when he left for being there and believing in me when no one else did.

"Thank God for your discerning mind, Mo. I hate to think what could have happened. We'll get this sorted out and he'll be okay. You've got a big day tomorrow. You're going to kill it. You all right?" I nodded. We kissed good night and I watched as what felt like the other half of my heart drove away. How I was supposed to sleep? I didn't have a clue but the drinks had calmed me down enough to get cleaned up and lie down.

I was running down a dark tunnel, I knew something was chasing me but I hadn't seen it yet. When I reached the end of the tunnel, a hand grabbed my shirt and pulled me to an abrupt stop. I turned in fear of what I might find. It was Danny. I sighed in relief.

"Dan," my dream image said, "What are you doing here?"

"I'm following you of course." He abruptly changed to red eyes and began to laugh maniacally. "I am hell, Montana. I am all your fears and I will swallow you whole but first I will start with your family...."

I awoke to sun streaming into my bedroom window. The security system Dan installed on the window brought my thoughts to him and the nightmare. Start with my family? "Not if I can help it," I mumbled to myself. Maybe old red eyes was pissed off because I had saved Dan before he had a heart attack.

I got ready for our first day in the studio. I was psyched to see it. Alex had been in while I was in Europe and said he had never felt so excited.

The place was huge and they had all state of the art equipment. Alex was like a kid in a candy store. He wanted to get into mixing and sound engineering as well so he listened to the rundown the engineer gave us and then he must have asked a thousand questions.

Otter and I were just taking it all in. This would be our home for the next several weeks. I couldn't believe how many people it took to put out an album. They had people in the sound booth, people running errands, people talking to back up singers, everywhere we looked there was activity around us.

"This is going to be awesome," Otter finally spoke. I laughed as I returned from a moment of stunned amazement. "Yes, it is gonna rock, just like us." I said, giving him a high five.

When it was time to begin, we spent a few minutes finding our groove, then the three of us started with the last song we had rehearsed yesterday. We felt our energies unleash and meld. We were ready. The sound engineers had us play all eight songs back to back before they started fiddling around with sound and feel.

We took a break, The potential back up singers were being tested. The engineers had them sing harmony with our music to hear the blend. The studio had provided us with lunch while we took our break. I noticed mine consisted of grilled salmon, and salad. Otter had a burger and Alex had a massive stir fry.

"Hey, who ordered the food?"

"I did," Alex answered.

"Well I want something different tomorrow. Why does Otter get a burger and I get fish?"

Alex grinned, "You'll have to take that up with your boyfriend, he told me what to order you."

Damn Adam, how did he have time to think of this stuff and act on it before I even knew it was happening. I muttered to myself about drawing the line. Then we ate in silence so we could hear the back up singers. We decided on the two we liked. Alex went and talked to the booth people and suddenly our band grew by two.

Studio playing was nothing like playing live. This was all nit-picky, perfection stuff, very tedious.

Alex, Otter and I finally left the studio at 5:00pm. It had been a long first day. We drove Otter home and went for a bite before heading over to the hospital to see Danny.

We arrived at the same time as Ace. "Do you know how he is doing?" I asked despondently, suddenly nervous about seeing him. Fatigue was starting to take me down.

"I phoned today and the doc said he is going through major withdrawal right now so we can't see him, but he should be through the worst of it in a few days.

Poor Danny. I wished I could hold him and tell him I loved him. We were just going into the doc's when Adam surprised us with his arrival.

"I had to come," he said. I squeezed his hand in silent support as we sat down in the doctor's office.

"I want to thank you all for coming. I am going to start with a short movie that explains what drug use does to the body so you know what Dan is dealing with and then I will be back to answer questions."

We watched the movie and when the doc came back Ace asked him what kind of time frame we were looking at with Danny.

"It depends on how quickly it leaves his system. Then, what kind of reactions he has to his cravings. After that, it is really up to him. If he decides to do drugs again then the process begins all over. It is not as addictive as heroin, having said that, he will face major urges and psychological withdrawals. The clearer he is on his purpose and who he is the better chance he has of moving forward and beyond his addiction.

Of course, association is critical as old habits are hard to break. The less he is around those that encouraged his habit the better. Often, recovering addicts must replace their obsession with something that involves adrenaline, like the gym or running. They need an endorphin replacement which is why working out is such a popular choice."

"Can we see him?" I asked.

"He is not himself, and he might not be for a few more days."

"I feel responsible."

"Don't feel bad Montana, he came in with so much in his system he could have had a heart attack. You did the right thing, even if it wasn't an easy thing to do. No promises, but we should have a better idea tomorrow." As it turned out, we still weren't allowed to see him the next day.

The day after that Alex and I went straight to the hospital after dropping off Otter. I'd had a bad day and more nightmares in between. I had to see Danny and make sure he was okay. I couldn't wait for Ace. They let us in and Alex stayed back allowing me a private moment with Dan. He was lying in bed, awake and moaning.

"Danny, it's me, Montana. Can I get you anything? Danny?" He heard me that time and looked my way. My heart ached seeing him so broken. I got a cold cloth and wiped the sweat from his brow and kissed his forehead, "I love you, Dan. I'm sorry if you're angry with me. Will you forgive me for making you come here?"

He didn't say anything and I was beginning to wonder if he was sleeping with his eyes open. I got some water. "Dan, drink some water." His glazed eyes turned my way, he blinked me into focus and allowed me to lift his head for some water.

"You never call me Dan." He attempted a smile, I gave him a hug and continued hugging him until it was time to leave. "I'll be back tomorrow," I promised, and we left. Dan's condition weighed heavily on my heart and my nightmares were so bad that night that Alex stayed with me.

Chapter 8

The next day at the studio we recorded our first song. Warm ups, practice runs, multiple takes, pickups, layers and layers until it all came down to the mixing. One song finished, complete and upon listening to it, perfect. I found it odd to hear our sound. I wouldn't have guessed in a million years that the band playing was us. I always zoned out when we played. I felt, rather than heard us.

A lunch break was called before we could begin to muddle through the next few. Alex was asked in to meet with the producer to discuss what we would be doing for the last few songs. I sat down with our new back up singers, Ann and Stella. They had lovely voices.

"Hi," I said. They said hi back. "I thought we should get to know each other better as we will be spending a lot of time together."

They seemed nervous but I loosened them up just chatting to them like we were old friends. By the time Alex came back the girls were laughing and feeling comfortable. I wasn't surprised when we recorded song two and we got it the first time through. Everyone was just into it, connected. We still had to layer tracks and double Alex's voice. By the time the mixing was done on track two it was nearly 4pm. We rehearsed some tunes for the next day's session to finish up.

We left the studio at 5:00pm., dropped off Otter, and grabbed a snack. "Is Ace meeting us?" I asked. "Yeah, and Adam I think."

"I can't wait to see Danny. I hope he is better today."

"How bad was he yesterday?"

"He just seemed totally gone... vacant, you know? Like he was dead in the head and he was sweating, which they said he would be. It was like he had the flu and brain damage at the same time."

Alex smiled, "You really have a way with words, Montana. Please don't ever describe me to anyone if I get sick." I laughed.

When we arrived at Danny's room Ace was already there sitting on the end of his bed and the two of them were laughing about something. We knocked. "Can we come in?" Alex and I said at the same time. They laughed again, and waved us in. Alex went over and gave Dan a big hug while I stayed at the foot of the bed, not sure how to proceed.

He seemed in his right mind, but, hey, it had only been a few days.

"What's the matter Mo, don't you have a hug for your big brother?" Sweet relief, I jumped on the bed and into his open arms.

"I am so glad you are doing better, you were so weird the other day. Actually, *you* weren't weird as much as the drugs made you weird."

"Montana, I am sorry, I don't remember anything. I must have been higher than a kite by the time you showed up at the studio. Ace told me what happened that afternoon and later when you guys came that night to get me. I don't know what to say to you. I was horrible."

"You're getting back to yourself and that is all that matters Danny. I gotta tell you though, you look like crap. You'd better clean up your act."

He laughed, "Yeah, well, I'm working on it." Adam hovered in the doorway until Danny spotted him. "Hey partner, I hear I gave you a boatload of work." Adam walked in and came over and they did the back slapping thing that guys do.

"Hey," Adam said, "I got everything from Jaimie-- the contracts and commissions that are up and coming, and I have combed through all the files. When you're feeling better I'll go over it all with you."

"Thanks Adam...for doing that." Adam smiled and nodded, no thanks needed he seemed to say.

"It's great to see you back to a more normal you," Adam said, focusing on the positive like he always did.

"I feel like roadkill but I'll live. Since the gang's all here, I have some things to say...the Doc said that if you had not brought me in that night when you did I probably would have had a heart attack. That is a huge wake up call for me. We just had this huge success and I turned into an instant idiot, a total amateur. I want you all to know how sorry I am...and how lucky I feel to have people like you..." he started to choke up and we all nodded and shuffled a bit as he sobbed a little and regained his composure.

"It's not all your fault," Ace spoke up to fill the gap. "We watched a video on drug use and 90% of users get started by someone they know. Association, they call it. We've let some people know they're not welcome anywhere near you again. I think we took care of your association problems for you. I hope you don't mind."

"You mean the dealer or Jaimie? I didn't even really know that guy... and Jaimie?" Adam shook his head, no. "Aww Jaimie...." Some of his inner grit started to come back. "Well, I just have to move on I guess. Maybe one day she will quit too." He softened, "Maybe I can help her out." His eyes looked haunted as he struggled with the realization that his love had become toxic.

"Maybe," Ace said, "but you're not seeing her for at least six months." Danny looked over at Ace. "These next six months will be the hardest for you and you can't afford the risk. Your heart can't afford the risk." Danny nodded slowly in agreement. I don't think he could have hung his head any lower if he tried. A nurse appeared in the doorway as a soft tone sounded. Adam prompted the next move.

"I meet with the record company in the morning. Alex, we should go over some ideas for the cover tonight and I can work on it in the morning before the meeting."

Visiting hours were over and we said our goodbyes and last hugs. When we were in the car I shared with Adam that it felt wrong leaving Dan there.

"It's good to see him doing better, but he is exactly where he needs to be and he is getting the best care. Dan needs this time to reconnect with himself. He has a lot to think about and he can't escape it in there." He was right, my feelings were just that, my feelings. But I wanted to fix things so badly!

The three of us went out and had dinner. Ace had wanted to come, but after laying it on the line for Danny, he just needed to be alone and headed home. Alex had the most ideas so he sat beside Adam, who sketched while they discussed them. We were all so worn out from confronting our busy schedules and caring for our recovering addict brother and partner. I spent the night with Adam at his apartment. I had missed him over the last few days, work and Dan had taken over our schedules.

There was something about Adam's place that I found really comforting. I had thought about it many times and was never able to put my finger on it. I was reclining on the couch with my feet up while he lit the candles, put on music and brought me a glass of wine. Right when he handed me my glass I said, "That's it!" and Adam almost dropped the glass.

"What's it?"

"I have been trying to figure out for months what it is about your place that I find so comforting."

"...And?"

"And, it's you, actually." He gave me a blank look. "This place is you. It's you Adam. You pervade this place. When I walk in here it is all so you. I have never been in someone's home that reflected them as much as yours does. It smells like you. I feel your comforting presence every time I walk in here. Isn't that cool?" My enthusiasm overwhelmed my eloquence.

"Yes, that is very cool." He chuckled.
Sometimes I felt like Adam was just patronizing me and he definitely needed to take a moment before he continued. After all, wine had nearly been spilt. "It's like when I enter your room at your house.... I find your smell so intoxicating. It's my favorite smell in the world--beyond comfort, it's like life to me."

"Awww, that is so special," I said, putting down my wine glass and moving closer to him.

He had deftly side-stepped making fun of me and continued with aplomb. "When I open one of my drawers here and I catch a whiff of you, I just want to hold you. But so often you are not here and I'm left having to make do with only your lingering scent."

He pulled me over the rest of the way, "How about we go and fill up your bedroom with the smell of me right now?" I said teasingly.

He grinned. "That is exactly what we are going to do." And he scooped me up, stopping at the candles so I could blow them out on our way to sensual bliss and sweet sleep.

Alex picked me up at 6:30am. and then we stopped and picked up Sir Otter, so we could get to work by 7:00. Work. What a strange word for what I got to do for a living. I played around on drums all day and because I made good money it qualified as work.

We would need 12 songs for the album. Two were done and we were hoping to get three done today. Now that the bugs had been worked out we had some idea of how to work in the sound studio. The more I was involved and heard the playbacks, the more I understood about the process. I realized why we would be big…we were tight. I overheard some of the sound mixers say that we were the best young talent to have come through in a long time.

Song three was done by lunch time when Adam arrived for his meeting. We took our lunch break since Alex would be in the meeting as well. Otter and I were called in to confer on the album cover. One of the things Ace and Alex had stipulated in the contract was that the players would have a say in all of the creative end of the band and its branding. We were to have total artistic control over the projects.

Adam had elaborated on the sketches he had made the night before and had come up with three that he felt best suited our wants; they were all great but one of them was more abstract. It had various scenes derived from our music, my lyrics and our past. I recognized Ralph in there and the funeral and dad and oil rigs, it was an artistic medley of what we were singing about on the album.

It was really cool. "I like that one," I said to Alex. He took a closer look and I knew he saw what I saw. It was subtly done, one of Adam's trademarks. A lot of work had been put into it when you stopped and really looked. Alex smiled at Adam and said to Richard the department head, "This is the one," as he passed it to Otter.

Otter looked at it for a while, then he smiled as he recognized what we saw. After the appointment I gave Adam a tour around the studio and introduced him to Stella and Ann. He liked the space and the gals, and when he left that day he had a cheque for $5,000 in his pocket. Not bad for one cover I thought. This world in which money flowed freely was beginning to seem normal.

Alex and I were the first to arrive at the hospital. Danny was sitting in a chair by the window looking out at the world. He seemed deep in thought, a small crease above his right eye the only evidence that he was a little forlorn.

We approached him. He was totally zoned out and didn't notice us. "Danny." He seemed to be coming out of a deep dream state, momentarily discombobulated.

"Hey... it's the famous Stanford twins," he finally got out. He stood unsteadily to give us a hug.

"How are you feeling, bro?"

"Okay. Feeling a little sad at the moment but good otherwise," he said.

"I brought you things to cheer you up, at least I hope they do. Your sketch pad and pencils, your Walkman and music and mom's diary. You expressed interest in it a while back so I thought you might want to take a read."

"Thanks Mo, I will read it." he said, placing the items on his bedside table. Ace walked in with some fast food for Dan.

"Oh man, I've been dying for this for days. I didn't eat when I was on the drugs. It takes away your appetite and since I've got it back all I could think about is a shake and a burger. Thanks bro." We laughed and watched him chow it down like a starving man.

"Dan, do you know when you can come home?" I asked.

"No, and I'm not pushing to get out early. It has been tough, but it's been good. I don't think I have sat still this long since I was ten and had that nasty flu. If I spend time reflecting it is usually while I'm painting, but just being here, in this situation.... I've had lots of time to think and I figured out the lure of the drugs, why I succumbed so quickly. It's weird, I had never even smoked a joint before I tried cocaine."

"Really?" I asked, incredulous. Ace gave me the look.

"The night of the gala I was giddy with the success of the show." Adam walked in while Dan was talking and stood by the door not wishing to interrupt.

Danny looked at Adam and addressed him directly. "You were always so cool when it came to the business side of art. I don't have a head for business. The success we experienced that night was so. . . intoxicating and for the first time I actually believed I was going to get somewhere.

Jaimie had all these art dealers and owners eating out of my hand and I remember the exact moment I felt the pressure of playing in the big leagues and not even knowing the rules of the success game. Adam was working the room in his quiet, efficient way and I felt so envious of you for the first time. That was the moment I became a pawn for every schmuck out there who wanted to rub shoulders with a new rising star. Then you and Montana left for Europe and my world fell apart," he admitted. "I'm really sorry. I could have totally screwed your career. If you want to branch out on your own, believe me, I will understand."

We all looked to Adam. He gazed back at Dan in that all seeing way of his. "I think you're stuck with me, Stanford. I can't create the new Group of Seven on my own now, can I?" I smiled at the reference, maybe using the name 'Stanford' would be an endearing thing in the future.

Dan visibly relaxed. I realized that this was probably what he had been thinking about when

Alex and I walked in, formulating his words to see if Adam still wanted him. When the visiting hours were over Adam and I left and went to dinner on our own.

Adam took me to a new restaurant up on tenth avenue, *The Elephant and Peach,* and the food was really good. It had a French twist to it that reminded me of a little bistro Adam and I had eaten at while in Paris.

"How is the recording coming?" he asked.

"Bloody tedious," I said, with a grin, "but I'm playing drums for a living so I can't' complain. I am lucky, a girl like me actually making it. My world isn't Shaughnessy, Adam. It's downtown, West End. Remember the fights I got into, the deceit, the broken ribs, being near death? That doesn't happen in everyone's life, especially in their childhood, so I guess I'm lucky."

"You're lucky all right. You've got a guardian angel looking over you. But more than that, I have never met a harder working family than yours. That night I was invited by your dad for the family dinner I was so impressed by him. His character and love for all of you and life, he seemed so fully alive. He instilled in all his children this incredible work ethic. If you didn't become successful after all he had poured into your life then it would have been your own fault not the society in which you lived."

I chewed on that over dessert. What he said was true. Perhaps I could be an example to all those who felt stuck and needed a hand up, maybe I could use some of the money I would make and start some type of program for teens. The direction of my thoughts excited me. Adam watched me and he smiled. I suddenly realized I wouldn't be having these kinds of thoughts if I didn't have him in my life.

"You know what?" I said.

"What?"

"You are the coolest person I have ever met."

"Thank you Miss Stanford."

I laughed at his formality. As we were walking out to the car I had another thought, "Adam, when you first met me did I live up to your expectations? Did I measure up to the descriptions that Danny gave of me?"

"You did, but he forgot to inform me that you are also enchanting."

"You think I'm enchanting?"

"Oh yes," he said. "You are the most enchanting little brat I have ever met."

"Ugh, you are terrible, you have been hanging around Ace too much. Can you not call me that for a while?"

He laughed as he opened the car door for me. "Very well m'lady." We went back to his place and I showed him just how enchanting I could be.

The following Friday Adam picked up Danny after work. I had requested that we get out of the studio a little early and I was now running around the house, ordering everyone around, trying to get things perfect for his return home.

Doreen the maid had been doing such an awesome job on the house that I decided to get her to do the grocery shopping as well. No one was home that much but it was nice to have a fully stocked fridge once a week.

Even though the house was clean, the guys had stuff laying around everywhere, so clean up involved me throwing clothes at everyone to put away. I was also busy with dinner, while the guys tidied.

Adam and Danny arrived. Ace put Danny's stuff in his room and we sat down to dinner complete with oddly shaped bottles of this new water on the market called Perrier. Conversation that night was focused around real estate; boring for me but the guys were into it so I listened while they talked about the pros and cons of the market and the outrageous interest on mortgage rates.

Danny suggested that we join forces and buy up property. "We are not all going to live together in this house forever and I think everyone here should be a home owner."

"I agree," Ace said, "but is the timing right? Everything could come to a head, level off and the market will have to drop. After all, with interest wars going on in the states right now, it' s bound to make its way up here too."

"My dad has a guy whose sole job it is to watch real estate investments. I could set up an interview for you guys if you want. I've got to tell you, the construction business is still booming and that is usually a good indication of how the market will go," Adam said.

"If you guys are almost done I would like to discuss me getting a vehicle." All eyes turned to me, I had their full attention.

"Danny has his mustang and Alex has his corvette. Adam has his new Porsche and you even have your old beater, Ace. I have all this money and no vehicle."

"What do you want to buy?"

"A mope head," You would have thought that I had just told a joke, they were howling with laughter even Adam. I realized it sounded ridiculous after I had just named off the cars that they had, but that was what I wanted.

When they finally stopped laughing, Ace said, "Montana you're not getting a mope head. You're not even going to get a moped. It is not practical and you can only drive it in the summer in our climate. You want a little something around you to give you a fighting chance should you ever be in a wreck.

"Okay," I pouted.

Conversation turned back to real estate. Alex was right into it. That figured, his brain was soaking up everything that was said. It occurred to me again that Alex was going to have it all; he was quietly ambitious and would own the world by the time we were done. He had the personality and the drive for it....

At dinner Ace had promised to take me car shopping on Saturday. True to his word, he showed me all kinds of cars, nice ones, but they just weren't working for me. Our last stop was the Volkswagen dealership and I saw the car I wanted. Ace wanted to argue at first because compared to what they all were driving what I wanted was not much better than the moped he said. His argument was doomed. Adam and I had rented one in Paris and I fell in love with it as he gave me lessons.

It was a Volkswagen cabriolet, beige interior and white on the outside, the roof was down. I was so excited I started jumping up and down chanting "this one, this one," over and over and Ace finally agreed. The dealer asked how we would like to pay for it and I looked him dead in the eye and said cash.

I drove my car off the lot feeling exuberant. I couldn't wait to show Adam. When he saw it he smiled and said, "I should have guessed that is what you would buy."

"Get in Northrop, I'm taking you for the first ride in my new baby." We drove up to the UBC area. The sun was out, it was a gorgeous day and I finally felt like an adult, completely independent. We parked by the woods and I thought of that day a long time ago when I had come here with Matt and we had that huge fight....

I laughed to myself at how much life had changed and how far I had come. We went down to Jericho beach after and just sat in the sun and had a coke. I was just starting to feel like life couldn't get any better when Adam said, "I have news."

"Mm-mm," was all I could muster. My body had gone to liquid butter in the warm relaxing sun.

"I am going to New York to meet with some art galleries. They heard about the success of our show and they are interested in having us out there. If it goes through then we will be painting our butts off for the next six months to finish off our commitments here and get ready for a show out there.... Which would really help us in the international market."

I sat up fully awake my sun coma gone. "Wow. Well. That is awesome news. Congratulations, when are you leaving?" As much as I wanted to sound enthusiastic it came out dry and whiney.

"Tomorrow," he said.

I chose to hold my tongue for a moment while I got my bearings. When I felt I could talk without pouting I asked for how long.

"I'll be home next Saturday. Can you stay out of trouble that long?"

I smiled, but something felt off. Somewhere in the distance somewhere red eyes heard and began to plot. I felt a shift in my destiny in that one simple sentence that Adam had spoken. *Could I* stay out of trouble for six days? I certainly hoped so.

"I'll do my best, but you know us brats. We always try but things just seem to pop up."

He didn't look as amused with my answer as I had hoped.

"I am telling you right now that she had better make me a promise and keep it, because if she doesn't, I will be getting her a full time babysitter."

I slugged him. "Don't be ridiculous, Adam. They don't have babysitters for adults."

"Well if you can't stay out of trouble for six days then you're not really an adult. Are you?" he said as he pulled me off the log and onto the sand into a warm embrace.

The next few days flew by and were filled with nothing but playing and refining and recording; basically, I ate and slept music. Adam had left and with time on my hands I invited one of our new backup singers over. Stella was exactly one year and one month older than me and she and I had really clicked. She had an interesting accent and I was curious to know more.

She thought the band rocked and she was looking forward to the touring. "Have you toured with anyone else?" I asked.

"Have you heard of the 'Sex Pistols?" I nodded, "I toured with them a bit when I was fourteen but my parents broke up my band when we moved over here."

"Holy smokes!" I replied, "What are you doing with us then? You should be out pursuing your own career not being our back up singer."

She smiled, "It will happen one day, I need a band first."

The light bulb came on, "I have an idea, Stella. I have friends that have a kick ass band, they should be ready next year to get moving with their career. When Alex starts his own record label, that will be the first band he signs. We know these guys and they could use a charismatic singer, it could be a great fit." She nodded her agreement.

"I will introduce you to them tomorrow if you want?"

"Sure," she said, "that would be bitchin'." Later that night I gave Cole a call and told him about Stella. He was excited to meet her, so I promised to bring her by and jam after we were done at the studio the next day.

As promised, the next day I took Stella up to meet Cole's band. They were rehearsing in his mom's garage. This brought back memories and I thought of Ralph and knew if he had still been around this band would be where we were now. He was a leader like Alex and had what it took to go all the way.

Stella and I listened to the guys for a bit. On a break, they asked if I wanted to jam with them. I said sure since I hadn't jammed with anyone but our band in forever.

I had grown as a musician and compared to me the guys came across rough around the edges and they knew it. Tim came over to me and shook my hand, "You're first rate, Mo. We've still got a ways to go".

"Thanks Tim. Don't worry, you're time will come."

It was now my turn to sit back and listen as Stella sang with them. As I had predicted she was perfect with them and gave them that extra bit they needed to make their sound come together.

Stella made an agreement to rehearse with them on the weekends and then we left.

"Montana," she gushed, "that was so cool. You're right they have the potential to be stellar."

I smiled, "Yep, and you're going to get big with them."

I dropped Stella off and then went for a drive. I was alone for the first time in days with my thoughts and feelings. I decided to drive around Stanley park and stopped at Ceperley Park playground for a swing. It felt great, feeling the wind in my hair, communing with the moon.

I hadn't done this in so long, nostalgic thoughts and feelings of my childhood filled me. It was some time before I left the park, probably around midnight by the time I got in my car. I saw a group of guys head out of the bushes down the road. I smiled, thinking of the things that I and my friends used to do in the bushes.

I drove off lost in my thoughts, and it wasn't until I was exiting the park that I noticed lights in my rear view mirror, right on my tail. I thought this was a 30 kmh. zone and I was already doing fifty. I sped up a little and went along Beach avenue. I turned left on Denman Street.

It didn't matter which way I turned they were right on my butt. I felt red eyes, these guys from the park weren't going to back off. They were following me on purpose. I turned down Comox street and pulled to the side to see if they would pass me. Instead, they parked right behind me and jumped out of the car.

I pulled out and made a U-turn heading back to Denman Street. But I didn't make it, the car stalled. I realized when I looked at the gauge I'd run out of gas. Damn.

I locked my doors. They were circling the car, cat calling me and telling me to let them in. I looked around for a weapon. All I had was an empty coke bottle so I grabbed the neck and kept it ready in my hand. Within moments, the soft top was being shredded as the back-side windows were being smashed in.

I felt arms grabbing at me. I struck an arm with the coke bottle and I heard someone howl and then yell a list of obscenities. I punched at another one and then the window of the back driver side broke and arms were dragging me back between the seats and then over the broken glass of the back window and out onto the street.

I was waving the bottle for all I was worth feinting and jabbing with my fist. The coke bottle was a decent bludgeon and a few heads were being tenderized. I wasn't going down without some of them coming with me. I was in complete adrenaline overload. They dumped me on the grass beside the car and circled me. I noticed some were bleeding out their noses and one was favouring what was likely a broken wrist.

Good. Whatever happened at least they'd have something to remember me by. I started to scream for help as they advanced on me. Someone behind me clamped their hand over my mouth. I bit down and tasted blood. Someone else punched me and I dropped the bottle, they were ripping at my clothes when I heard sirens.

Thank God, someone had called the police. Two got away but two others were caught. They were being hauled off while I gave my story and got patched up by paramedics. I was congratulated on my self defense skills but I was still pissed they got any shots in.

"I have three brothers who taught me how to defend myself."

"I have your statement," Officer Collins said, "and I will call you tomorrow if I need anything else. Montana Stanford, I know that name." I told him he had most likely seen me or one of my brothers in the papers. We'd had our share of publicity lately.

He nodded his head. "My wife is an art fan. She has been following Danny Stanford's work." He gazed at me and asked if there was anyone I wanted him to call. I was about to answer no, I was fine, when who should walk around the ambulance but Eddy, my buddy the cop. He was dressed in plain clothes as he was now a detective.

He looked surprised, then not so surprised. Officer Collins said his goodbyes as Eddie said he would make sure I got home.

"Jesus, Mo, are you okay? They said some cute little tough thing with a bottle held off a bunch of guys. I should have bloody guessed it would be you," he said, grabbing my arm and steering me around to the back of the squad car where we could talk in private.

"What were you doing at Ceperley by yourself at this time of night?" he asked, crossing his arms and gazing down at me. I wasn't in trouble but he would get my full confession. However, instead of confessing I began to cry. The shock of what had just occurred set in.

He drew me into a hug, and held me until I calmed down. He signaled to the remaining officers that he was taking me home. He also arranged to have my car towed to the dealership so they could repair the damage.

He drove to my place and I told him about my day. I explained that I had no intention of stopping when I started my drive around the park but when I saw the swings I felt a pull. I parked to enjoy the quiet and my thoughts.

Eddy came in with me when we arrived at the house. Ace was going over paper work so he didn't look up as he spoke.

"Hey Montana, you're in late, get into any trouble?"

He meant it as a joke but when no response was forthcoming he glanced up to see Eddy and me in the doorway. The blood on my forehead got his attention.

"Christ girl, what has happened to you now?" he said, rising and coming over to us.

"Let's have a drink," Eddy said," and we'll go over the story. There are things Mo doesn't know yet about her assailants."

Ace brought us all a hefty glass of whiskey, I began the tale and Eddy took over from when the police arrived.

"So here is the issue," Eddy said, putting down his glass. "We've been trying to nail this gang for a while. The ring leader is well connected in Chinatown. He got out of prison about a week ago. This group of guys is notorious for rape and murder. We have never found a victim alive or willing to testify so we haven't been able to arrest and prosecute them."

"Excuse me," I said, as I ran to the bathroom where I threw up my whiskey. It was just as yucky coming up as it was going down. Maybe a little yuckier. Eddy continued when I came back.

"They have never been convicted of anything more than petty theft. The special crime lab has been working up a profile against them, but so far they have been able to elude us. They've all done time so they're in the system, but Montana is our first chance to put any of these guys away."

Oh God. Of course I am. Why? I yelled at myself. Why did I have to be there tonight? Because of red eyes, that was why.

"Do you think they were randomly following Montana or was it intentional?"

"It's really hard to say at this point, Ace. She fits the profile of their other victims. I can't ignore the possibility that Mercy is responsible for this attack. One thing I will tell you, if we can put away even two of them we can apply pressure and start to control things in Chinatown."

"So, how does this work? Do we all have to testify against them so they get locked up?"

"Montana, you're not hearing me. You are the only victim or witness we have. Although if you testify perhaps others will come forward, at this point you're it. As far as what you do next? Nothing until we can confirm everything and have a case. Most likely you will be asked to go downtown tomorrow and identify your attackers in a line up. Once you confirm them, they will be booked. We will figure out our next move after that. In the meantime if you start to feel like you are being watched or see anything unusual you need to phone me or the police."

With that, Eddy left and Ace and I were left to ponder what we had been told. Suddenly, I remembered Adam's threat.

"A penny for your thoughts, Mo."

I sighed, "I was just thinking about what Adam said before he left for New York."

"Oh…and what did he say?"

"That if I got into any trouble he was going to hire me a professional babysitter."

Ace thought that was hilarious and laughed for quite a while. "I sure like Adam," he finally got out. "I should have thought of that years ago."

"Let's not tell him," I pleaded. "Let's just keep this whole incident between us."

He just gave me the look. This one meant 'if you say another word you're not going to like where you end up.'

I dropped the subject. Ace took a pragmatic approach. "I'm glad you're okay. As far as the rest goes, we will deal with it in steps like we always do."

I nodded and headed off for a shower and then to bed.

Montana…Montana…where do you think you are running to? You can't escape me. I am coming for you, can't you see? You're not safe anywhere. Why do you bother fighting me? Everyone dies and you will have to watch…. Look into my eyes…don't you know me?

I awoke the next morning screaming. This time it was Danny who came flying into my room. Alex had stayed late at the studio and I wasn't sure if he even came home.

"Mo, what's going on?"

"I have been having these nightmares for months, since before Adam and I left for Europe. I get an omen that something bad is going to happen, then it does...and now I'm afraid something horrible is coming and I can't stop it." He held me while I cried it out of my system. He said nothing but he watched me during breakfast. He seemed as if he wanted to share something but every time he went to speak he stopped himself. When Ace entered the kitchen, the conversation shifted to safety.

My car was toast for a few days while they replaced windows and cleaned it up, so I drove to work with Alex who took one look at me and just rolled his eyes and mumbled something about me being reckless and that was it. After work I was requested down at the police station and Alex must have really been getting into learning the sound board because he let me go without a word.

Alex didn't understand as I hadn't shared last night with him and neither had Ace. However, Ace did meet me and Eddy at the station after work to give moral support while I identified my attackers in the lineup.

"Its them Eddy," I said feeling a little faint.

"Will you testify Montana?"

"Eddy, what I do know? It's not just about me, but the effect on the band and our future. I guess I should get some council and see what the label has to say. I would like to because I think they are animals and should be put away. But I also feel that this needs to be run by the studio and Alex."

"Even if we can't directly link the other attacks and murders, they will go to prison for a long time based off their rap sheet and your testimony."

"Who did they murder?" I asked.

"All the vics were young females between 18 and twenty who were raped and then beaten to death." I felt sick. For the moment, the police force would have to be satisfied with the suspects being identified. The rest would follow on the heels of advice I would seek from the label and Alex on Monday. It was Friday and I needed to go and pick Adam up at the airport.

Ace dropped me off at Adam's place so I could get his car. I thought of some bogus story I could say to him that would explain the stitches and the missing car... and then what? It had been on the news, his parents or Dan would tell him... or someone. I needed to come clean. Ugh, I hated that. It was so painful I was squirming just thinking about it.

I decided to wear my jeans and a t-shirt and my baseball cap so it covered the stitches on my head and the t-shirt was long sleeved so you couldn't see the stitches there either. His plane was early. He was already out front when he saw me pull up in his Porsche. I jumped out and gave him a big hug.

"I missed you so much," I said. He laughed.

"It's only been a week. Hey, where is your car?" he asked, as he put his bag in the trunk.

"Oh... some kid threw a rock through my window. So, it is in getting repaired."

"Really?"

"No."

He frowned, "No?"

"No, that is not true. I have a story, um…to share with you." He didn't say anything, just did that staring through me thing that made me squirm.

"I'm driving," he finally said and hopped in the driver's seat.

Chapter 9

I didn't want to talk about it while he was driving so I asked him how the meetings went.

"I will tell you my news-- after you tell me yours. You know you're not supposed to drive my car unless you ask first."

The rest of the ride was spent in silence. When we arrived at his house, he threw his stuff in his room while I poured wine. We sat down on the couch. I was already turning red and I hadn't even started speaking yet.

"Well?"

I took off my cap and showed him the stitches. Adam, who had never been seriously hurt, always flinched when he saw my injuries. Then I pushed up my sleeve and showed him the other wound.

"Oh Montana," he sighed, drawing me in for a hug, "does it hurt?"

"It did, but it doesn't bother me so much right now."

"Start with when, where and why."

"A few days ago, at Ceperley Park. I was alone, I needed to be alone."

"That park is packed all the time. Didn't anyone see anything?"

"It was late at night. After I dropped off Stella I had been pushing myself in your absence so I just wanted to hang out and unwind a bit. I felt safe in my old stomping grounds so when I saw a group of guys exit the bushes a ways down from me I didn't think much of it. I jumped in my car and left the park. They followed me.

I stopped to see if they would keep driving past me. They jumped out of their car and I tried to leave, but wouldn't you know, I was out of gas. I had a coke bottle in the car so I used it as a weapon. I held my own for a while and I screamed bloody murder. I guess somebody heard because the cops arrived before anything nasty happened.

Eddy was also at the crime scene. He told me that these guys may be connected to Mercy as they belong to the same Chinatown crime boss. It may have been coincidental or I may have been targeted, they don't know yet.

I identified the ones they have in custody, but two got away. If I testify they will go to jail. They have done this before. Um, the other women they did this to were all killed with no witnesses. I am the only one to have survived an attack by this group. They need me so these guys don't do this to anyone else. I haven't decided yet. I wanted to talk to you and Alex and the label to consider the possible ramifications."

He sat back and slowly exhaled.

"I don't know what to say to you right now. Part of me is terrified, and part of me wants to tan your hide for being so bloody stupid. Mostly," he said, "I am grateful you are alive and here with me to tell the tale."

He drew me in and held me tight.

"You're getting a body guard," he murmured in my ear.

"What? You will do no such thing. You can't," I said, standing and pacing the room.

"I most certainly can and will. And you're not driving either."

"Adam!"

"Listen to me. I care about you and you're going to have a bodyguard. Don't even think about trying to give him the slip, or I'll tie you to a chair and cart you around myself."

"You're just like Ace," I said accusingly.

"Good thing for you that I am," he barked. "You seem to have the devil after you and I am keeping you alive damn it. Whine all you want to, it isn't going to change my mind."

This was not how I wanted things to be between us. I needed to change direction.

"Adam, please tell me about your trip."

"I'm really angry with you right now. Let me have a shower, then we can talk about the trip. He headed off to the shower and I relaxed on the couch with my wine. When he came back and joined me, I asked if it was okay to talk now....

He pushed my hair back and looked at my forehead and shook his head, "What did Ace have to say?"

I went beet red.

"He thought the babysitter idea was hilarious and he said he should have thought of that years ago."

Adam smiled, "What else did he say?"

"He said he would have grounded me for life but it was unrealistic given my situation."

"And?"

"And what?"

"What else did he say?"

"Oh for Pete's sake, aren't you tired of wondering what he said? Why don't you just ask him?"

He gave me the Ace look.

"Oh fine." I said, "He said, I'm stupid, reckless and irresponsible." I mimicked Ace perfectly as I said it. Adam laughed.

"Okay, okay enough." I jumped on his lap. "Tell me you love me." He was trying to do his angry look again but I was wearing him down.

"Come on," I said as I kissed his entire face. I was slowly moving to his neck when he said, "Have I ever told you that you make me nuts sometimes?"

"Join the club, we have jackets," I replied in a muffle as my lips were busy. He moved me back on the couch and kissed me deeply, a truly passionate and loving kiss. Events from that point unfolded more to my liking.

The next day I met Charlie. He was huge. He made Ace look small. Charlie was my new bodyguard and would be for as long as I needed one, according to Adam. The timing was good as everyone knew that our band was blowing up and while Alex handled his fans well, I needed all the help I could get. At the studio, only Alex knew the real reason for Charlie's employment while the investigation was open and court cases were pending.

Thus began my days with Charlie the giant. He was actually a nice guy. He told me he had been a body guard for some huge musicians including Steven Tyler from Aerosmith. I guess it was a compliment that Adam had secured him for me.

The band was getting ready to leave on tour. I felt isolated by the idea of being away from Adam.

"Adam, I'm starving can we get a pizza and snuggle on the sofa with a blanket and watch a movie?"

"Sure, tonight it's whatever you want. Tomorrow is another story but tonight, whatever you want."

"Adam, how am I going to live without you for 8 weeks?"

"You will be so busy most of the time, living on a very controlled schedule, you won't have time to miss me. Besides, you can write me any time, and call me when you get to your hotel wherever you are."

I sighe   d. S o he said, but it wasn't enough. I had no idea how this whole tour thing would play out. I knew Alex would handle it with grace and Otter would be fine. As for me, who the hell knew?

We ate our pizza and watched Eddy and the Cruisers and fell asleep on the couch.

The next morning Adam took me home to finish packing for the tour. We were leaving on a red eye that night. Our tour was beginning in Poland, then the USSR, Sweden, Denmark, Germany, Austria, Czech Republic, Italy, Greece, France, Spain, Ireland, Scotland, and England.

When we arrived at the airport we were ushered down to a separate terminal and out to a chartered plane. The company was flying us with a small entourage that included a stage manager, hair makeup and a few roadies. Charlie showed up to take care of me on the road.

We were new and with the record launch in Europe earlier that summer there was time to create momentum and get people in a lather about seeing and hearing "*Behind Blue Eyes*."

We landed in the early morning in Warsaw. I didn't see much of it, only what I saw out the window from the airport to the hotel. We promptly checked in and I went to sleep. We had to be at the Torwar Hall in the afternoon for final sound checks and to go over the set up.

Makeup and hair and costume would be done there so we needed to be showered and ready. I was a bundle of nerves as we made our way to the hall. It was not a huge place compared to stadiums I'd seen shows in before, it held about five thousand people, but it was way bigger than anywhere we'd played yet. A good place to start the tour as the audiences would get bigger from there.

The reviews on the record had been very positive in Europe. Our singles had massive air play on the radio and they were selling like crazy in the stores. Our first concert had sold out. We re-did our stage set up a few times with Alex making sure everything was perfect, while Otter and I watched, rum and cokes in hand.

Sound checks were done several times to get out the bugs and then I went into hair and makeup and wardrobe. I needed more time than the guys. The studio and Alex had decided to brand us with a specific look. The guys were in black and I was in white. I looked like an extension of my drum kit with a flourish of dark hair.

It was time. I floated over to my drum kit, very much feeling like I was having an out of body experience. The guys picked up their instruments. The stage was dark so the crowd couldn't see us but they knew we were there and a thunderous applause began accompanied by shouts in a language I didn't understand so I had no idea what they were saying.

The anticipation was brutal. I thought I was going to puke, and then we began. I was too aware of our surroundings, and the fans, and the seriousness of the situation. We needed to kill it, the success of tonight would beget the success of the next location, and so on. Then I remembered my own advice to Alex after we signed the contract…they liked us for who we are already, just relax and be yourself.

And with that thought I took off. I let go, just like driving with no hands, I let go of the tension, the expectation, all of it. The three of us became a tight, grooving machine and they loved us. We played two encores and then just like that we were done. I was laughing as we exited the stage.

Alex grinning said, "Did I miss something? What is so funny?"

I had tears pouring out of the corners of my eyes I was laughing so hard. I wheezed out finally that I couldn't $#%*& believe that we made so much #$%&* money for having that much fun. Alex joined in the laughter and that is how Otter found us moments later, hanging off each other until we were wrung out with amusement.

We were given some time to clean up and freshen up and then we were taken to the backstage party. This was new for me. Playing a concert meant there were backstage passes, like the show after the show for those willing to pay the big bucks. My inclination was to hide in my personal dressing room until everyone went away. I was informed by the stage manager that that was not acceptable, so instead I stuck with Alex.

He did his thing and I nodded and smiled. We signed plenty of autographs: t-shirts, albums, you name it. Arms, hands, I was even asked to sign with permanent marker on someone's butt. Alex and Otter were surrounded and looked like they were in their glory although few of the fans spoke much English. They mainly chanted our song lyrics at us and passed drinks while they smoked. Everybody smoked!

Alex did the rounds. He spent time with the press answering many questions. One reporter was a beautiful young Japanese woman. There was an instant attraction between her and Alex. I swear I saw arrows pierce them both at the same time.

Naturally, Alex spent the remainder of his time engaged with Allyson, the reporter. Otter and I did our best to keep up whatever it was we were supposed to be doing. Someone passed me a joint, so I motioned to Otter and we disappeared into my dressing room with the joint.

We each had a few tokes and totally destressed. "I don't know how he does it," Otter said. I knew what he meant.

"Me either, and he seems to enjoy it."

"He sure likes that Asian gal, eh Mo? What's her name?"

"Allyson," I answered, "and I'm sure it's mutual. I was watching both of them when they were introduced and it looked like love at first sight to me."

With the edge off, Otter and I were ready to face the crowd again. When we rejoined the party, we were ready to participate. We drank and danced and whooped it up while Alex remained with Allyson looking like they were having some earnest conversation about who knows what.

I did see him glance our way from time to time. I knew we had to be on the road early and he was probably trying to determine how much steam we would have if we didn't get out of there soon. I was having a great time now and Otter and I were cracking up at the funny mistakes people were making with our lyrics.

I decided I really liked Poland. The young people there really knew how to have fun. I was getting ready to smoke some more pot when Charlie (who had discreetly remained in the background up until then), said it was time to go. There was no arguing with the friendly giant. He got me out of there, with Alex and Otter.

I was pretty far gone, and feeling cheeky.

"Hey Charlie, who's paying you for this babysitting gig the studio or Adam?"

"Both," he answered.

"So, what? The studio is paying you and Adam is paying you to keep him updated on how I am doing?"

He gazed at me in his somber, impassive way but said nothing. I decided to call Adam and ask him myself when we arrived at the hotel. He answered on the second ring, "Hey, how's it going?" he asked.

I slurred my words, "Adam, did you hire the GIANT to report back to you on my... behavior?"

Silence on the other end. "Having a good time darling?" he asked dryly.

"Hmmph, yessiree.... Jim Dandy and all that. Yep." I was quickly losing interest as he was giving me nothing to yell about so in my stupor I said, "Goooodnight," and hung up.

Oh God. 9:00 am came way too early and I was hungover. I had breakfast and showered and packed and headed down to the lobby with the giant. "Morning Charlie," I said.

"Morning Miss Stanford," he answered. I grimaced at him. He knew I hated being called Miss Stanford.

We were off to the USSR for two shows and a repeat of last night. I hoped not a total repeat. I felt horrible. I had time for an hour nap before getting ready and heading down for sound checks. I tried calling Adam before I left but there was no answer, so I left him a message letting him know that we were in Kiev and I would talk to him after the concert.

I wasn't as nervous this time. Tonight I felt like here we go again. The crowd went wild, and we nailed it as usual. The after party was more crazy if that is possible. It's like nothing was illegal in these places and people were doing things that I had never seen in Canada. Of course, I was always protected by my brothers and heck, I was still a teenager.

Allyson had followed us on the tour so Alex was busy. Otter and I went and smoked something that someone passed to us and were just coming out of my dressing room when a wildly dressed couple came up and the woman asked me if I wanted to go party with them back at their place. I looked at these charismatic crazies with their broken English but there was no doubt what they intended as the woman started touching me while her boyfriend groped her. Just then, I spotted Adam.

I saw him looking around for me, and I felt the moment he found me. I froze. Otter was out in the crowd partying it up. I pretended not to see Adam and headed to the other side of the party, couple forgotten, hoping he would just wait out his time and give me a chance to think about what to say to him. Why was he here anyway? He didn't trust me, that's why he was here.

Well, if that was it then it was time to confront him. I grabbed a drink and went looking for him. He was talking to Charlie, damn him. He saw me approach and redirected me to my dressing room, where I didn't want to go as it reeked of pot.

"Why are you here?" I asked.

"It's nice to see you, too. Hiding in here and smoking pot, really? When did that become part of your routine?"

"Adam, I'm eighteen years old, in a few months, what is the big deal?"

"The big deal is, you're acting thirteen not almost eighteen. This is not your first show. You know better. At this rate you will be burnt out by next week and doing what exactly? What Dan did?"

I felt instantly ashamed. I was acting like a total amateur and falling into the same trap that Dan had fallen into. "You're right." I said. "I haven't been thinking, just acting. I'm sorry."

"We're going back to the hotel. I will manage your time for the next few days while you figure it out."

"But Adam, you can't. I have a contract you can't just change things. Please rethink this. I don't want to look like a baby." My thoughts were scrambled eggs. He was right. The only problem was I was higher than a kite.

"I can't stay with you on this entire tour. I have a few days and then I have to get back. It can either be great or not. Either you learn some control or you're going to have it taken away. You're a minor, you will do what you're told." We left then and got into a stretch limo back to the hotel.

I gave up the fight and leaned my head onto his chest. "I'm tired daddy, can we go to bed?" He held me for a few minutes. I relaxed feeling his solidness beneath me. When we arrived at the hotel he helped me to bed and I was out like a light..

I woke to find breakfast waiting for me. I ate like a starving person. Adam was in the shower, evidence said he had already eaten. He exited the bathroom while I put down my fork after my last bite. He sat down on the bed with me and we had coffee and talked about how things were going.

"What did you tell Dan?" I asked, as I took a sip of my coffee, unwilling to make eye contact.

He grinned. "I told Dan that I needed to see my muse before going to New York," he responded lifting my chin to look in my eyes.

"So, you didn't tell him what I've been up to?"

"No, we have a few hours before leaving for Moscow, what do you want to do?"

My eyebrows lifted, "Really? Do you need to ask?" The last of the USSR concerts went smoothly. As much as I resented being babysat, Adam was great company. Having a skilled personal masseur and lover helped my stress levels immensely.

We travelled the next morning to Sweden. We arrived before everyone else, checked in and had a wonderful meal. Thankfully, the band wasn't playing until the next evening allowing Adam and I some down time to stroll through the cobbled streets of Stockholm.

That night we had dinner with Alex, Otter and Allyson. I had told Adam about her and the sparks between her and Alex when they first met. I knew he wanted to check her out and see what was what, maybe even get Geoff to run a background check on her.

We went to Mancini's, a five-star Italian restaurant and it was fabulous. We had amazing wine and food, and both Adam and I really enjoyed Allyson. She was from a wealthy Japanese family who had sent her to the U.S. to study journalism.

She had landed a job upon graduation with Maximum Rock n Roll out of San Francisco, and had been with them a year now. Allyson was intelligent, well-educated, wealthy, and older than Alex and I by a few years.

"She's like the female version of you," I said to Adam later that night after making love.

"Oh, and why is that?"

"Really? Rich, only child, best schools, you know, spoiled rich kid stuff." I laughed until Adam smothered my mouth with his and Allyson was forgotten....

Adam left the next day and the next several weeks flew by. I phoned him every night after the gigs. Alex kept a better eye on me since Allyson had run out of excuses to stay and had headed out as well. She would meet up with us in Vancouver after the tour for a little R&R. Charlie had had nothing to report to Adam and had grown a little bored with his assignment. I told him to cheer up, there were worse places he could be.

We were in our last week of touring and we were in England. It was the end of November and the weather had gotten nasty. I got a cold and was feeling miserable. We had three nights there before heading home.

As the studio had planned, our success had preceded our arrival in London. When we arrived there were crowds at the airport, fans outside our hotel, and fans everywhere you looked. I tried to be kind but I felt like shit and all I wanted to do was lie down. Adam and Danny were in France and scheduled to meet us in London the next night.

I signaled to Alex that I was heading up to my room. He nodded while he and Otter kept signing autographs. Charlie and I headed up to my room. He and I had been getting on well since I cleaned up my act.

We both saw a gift in my suite on the table. It was heavy for such a small thing. Opening it I saw a picture of flaming red eyes. I felt as if I would pass out but there was something beneath the photo so I started to move the picture aside. It was a little stiff so I pulled. Charlie saw my expression and charged across the room towards me as I gazed at a small pineapple shaped grenade inside the box. I looked at the back of the picture and saw the separated pin firmly attached.

"Don't touch that!"

Everything seemed in slow motion after that…Charlie grabbed the bomb from my hands, turned away and threw it out the open balcony doors using his spinning momentum to face me. Before it traveled very far it went off. I caught a glimpse of the flash as Charlie dove backwards onto me, propelled by the explosion behind him.

"Montana, Montana, can you hear me?" I tried opening my eyes but the light hurt. I could hear but my head felt like it had exploded. I moved my hands to my ears and moaned. "Hang in there Mo, the ambulance is on its way." I rolled towards where the balcony had once been, now just an open gaping maw. I stared in confusion at the scene. Nothing made any sense.

Security was everywhere. Charlie was sitting up with his head in bloody hands, looking at me from a few feet away, so he wasn't dead, thank God. The leather jacket he always wore had been destroyed and his back was a bloody mess. I waved at him and he nodded slightly. Alex was leaning over me.

"What happened?" I asked him. Apparently I was shouting. Sound shimmered like cellophane and echoed into my brain as if reverberating through a drum full of water. Ha. Drum...

"Stop yelling. It's okay Mo, the explosion alerted everyone and the only damage below is to the sidewalk. The people managed to scatter in time. Just you and Charlie were injured. Lay still, the paramedics are here."

"Temporary ear drum damage," I heard someone say to Alex. "Some scrapes, bumps and a few stitches and some anti-inflammatories. She should be fine but we will know better after we run some tests." I was put on a stretcher and carried away. The paramedics used the staff elevator that took them into the underground parking. Alex followed Charlie, who had been examined and was also being placed on a stretcher. They'd need four people to carry him. A few reporters had managed to get through security and were snapping pictures. I felt the bulbs like fiery spears in the backs of my eyes.

Alex was livid and shouting at security to do their damn job and remove the scum immediately. If I could have smiled I would have. It was so funny hearing him sound like Ace, or Adam….

Oh Adam. This would be on the news and he would be so upset.

"Alex," I moaned, "call Dan. Tell him I'm okay and not to worry. Tell him to take care of Adam. I will be fine."

I must have passed out after that for the next thing I remembered was waking up in a lovely hospital room, my brother on the chair beside me talking to someone. He felt rather than saw I'd returned to consciousness and hung up the phone.

"Tell me I'm fine," I said almost desperately.

"You're fine."

"I am?" Alex turned and met my eyes.

"Not really. The doctors have run tests, we are waiting on the results now. There is some swelling in your ears, but they feel it will be gone within a week. However, right now it is critical that you rest or the swelling won't go down. Do you have a headache?"

"Don't talk so loud. It's not as bad as before. I felt like my head had exploded."

"You are so lucky. Charlie saved your life. Adam will be giving him a big bonus, no doubt."

"How is Charlie?"

"Like you, but he had some flesh wounds to his back from the explosion and he broke a few ribs. He's not feeling good, but he was lucky as well. Parts of the furniture went through the walls on either side of you guys. He's got fancy bandages and stitches in a few places but he tested fine. He joked about all the years of rock music protecting his ears and then he booted everybody out so he could call home about something."

"And Adam?"

"He and Dan are on their way…. Mo, what was in the box on top of the bomb? Charlie said you were holding something else."

"Yes, I was. In the top of the box was a picture…of red eyes."

"Holy shit, are you serious?"

"Yes."

Chapter 10

It would be a few days at least before I could travel home. The Doctors were monitoring the bruising in my ears. The band had no choice but to cancel our last two dates in London. Alex had offered to bring in another drummer but they wanted to have the 'whole' band so we postponed our dates until the new year. The company expressed their regrets and condolences, but they couldn't have bought this much publicity if they spent millions on it. We'd be back.

Adam had rented us a large furnished flat in a hotel that lay within the hospital district making our trips to and from easy and painless. It took two days for the ringing in my head to quiet enough that I could speak with Eddy on the phone.

He wanted to know every detail of what I could remember about the picture and the bomb in the seconds I saw them both. He'd spoken with Charlie already to gather any other details his trained security mind may have picked up.

I agreed to press charges against the two attackers who had been caught. Eddy felt that the two who had escaped had orchestrated the bomb. With me dead, I couldn't testify against their partners who in turn may give up the identity of the others in exchange for a reduced sentence.

The entire incident was not only terrifying but the implications were far reaching. The bomb could have killed the entire band and the crew who had toured with us, in addition to all the other innocents that were staying on our floor. And perhaps the floors below and above. Had there been children staying near us? I didn't know but the idea made me ill. It was hard for me to fathom that a simple car ride and midnight swing had caused so much trouble. I questioned my decision making and my integrity.

I rested and slept a lot. The nightmares came and went but they no longer seemed prophetic. I felt they continued because the trouble was far from over as long as my life was tied to the gang. I wasn't the only one who was stunned by their brazen actions. Adam and I still hadn't talked about what had happened yet. The bomb had left me feeling resigned and sad. Resigned in that I had no control, sad that no one did. Effecting a positive outcome was far from a reality.

I could tell Adam was concerned with our lack of communication. He didn't push. It wasn't until our last evening in London that I was ready to talk. We sat down to dinner in our suite. He had an amazing meal brought in complete with candles and wine. He created a relaxed subdued setting and his efforts paid off. He filled my glass.

"I am ready to talk. How is Charlie doing?"

"He's recovering back in Vancouver. The medical care here is stellar but he would only let them patch him up and demanded a specific surgeon he's known for a long time once he was stable enough to fly. A few weeks of healing and he says he'll be ready to get back to work."

"Really? I thought he would have run for the hills."

"I offered to let him resign from babysitting duty but he would have none of it. He said working as your bodyguard was more exciting than any other gig to date. He will be ready and waiting for your return to the studio."

I smiled, and my eyes watered a little as my heart filled with gratitude for Charlie the giant. "I'd be dead without him."

"Yes, you would." Adam responded.

"Have you spoken to Alex, did he tell you what I told him?"

He nodded.

"How is it possible Adam? I did not conjure those red eyes from my imagination. I couldn't have made it up. I'm just thankful that all the threats in my nightmares did not come true. Maybe it's black magic. How could my subconscious come up with something so improbable?"

"I don't know Mo. It's beyond my scope of understanding. You haven't dreamt anything about this dinner, have you?" It was a good line but I just shook my head as we continued our meal in silence.

"On a different topic, Alex called to let you know the record was released in Canada yesterday. I realize it's difficult to find the silver lining in this situation but the media publicity from the bomb has propelled your sales through the roof. Alex says he is a hunted man. He can't go anywhere without being peppered with questions and asked for an autograph."

"I bet he is in his glory. He does love attention." I paused, wondering how he would take my next comments. "I have been questioning myself Adam. This attack has had me thinking a lot this week."

He nodded in response.

"I realize that to blame myself for all that has occurred would be fruitless. So, I have decided to not do that. Christmas is two weeks away. I want to use the holidays to put what has happened in London behind us. Do you think we could still go through with the idea of Christmas in the harbour of Vancouver Island?"

Adam's eyes sparkled. I had no idea why. His response was noncommittal. He said he would look into the idea, but no promises.

We flew home the next day, it was a long ten-hour flight. When we landed there was a small security team there to meet us. Charlie was among them. Though not officially back, he wanted to greet us. I smiled when I saw him. Feeling the bloom of gratitude in my heart I gave the giant a gentle hug. "Thank you, Charlie, I wouldn't have made it without you." He patted me lightly on the back, clearly not a man for soft moments.

We headed out of the airport and for home. The first thing I did was flop down on my bed. I loved that bed. The next day I stayed in my pajamas and puttered from the kitchen to my bed. I think the guys were worried about my state of mind. I was quiet, unusually so. I was exhausted.

I knew they were worried, but I was fine. At least a part of me was totally fine. The other, I kept a tight lid on. I didn't want to think about London. I could still feel the impact of the explosion, the unreality of the situation and how close to death I'd come.

Adam had a special dinner planned for me the next evening. I was told we were celebrating privately so to wear something to suit the occasion. I dragged my butt out of bed and Alex and I went shopping at the Leather Ranch on Granville Street.

I bought a tight, curve hugging red leather mini-dress and over the knee black leather boots.

I made my grand entrance when he arrived to

pick me up. I received the jaw dropping reaction I was looking for. Just as I was doing a 'for your eyes only' bump and grind to show off my curves, Danny walked in the room and stopped dead in his tracks. He gave a whistle, "looks like you're in trouble tonight buddy," he said, chuckling.

Adam blushed. That was a first. We left to Dan's laughter and got in the Porsche. "Where are we going?"

"Never you mind, it' s a surprise."

"What are we celebrating?"

"Montana, we are young and rich. We are always celebrating something."

I smiled, "That's true, but are we celebrating something in particular?"

"Yes, we are."

"Oh goody! I love it when we celebrate something in particular, what is it?"

"Stop asking. I'm not telling and you'll find out soon enough. But I would like you to wear this blindfold until we get there."

"This is kinky. You're not going to play some rotten trick on me or anything, are you?"

I gave him a hard look before I covered my eyes.

"If I was, I certainly wouldn't tell you."

He switched the conversation to money and he went on and on. What he had created and what he was worth, blah, blah, blah. "I know Adam, but I promise not to hold all your wealth against you."

"Okay Miss Cheeky, let me finish my spiel," he continued. "I have already made over a million dollars with my art in these last few months--"

"Yeah, thanks to me being your muse."

"One more word and no surprise," he said, attempting to sound stern.

He parked and we walked down what felt like a wharf. I smelled the sea and heard lapping and knew we were in a marina. Now I was curious, what was he up to?   We halted and he removed my mask. "Oh Adam, it is incredible!"

Adam and I had talked so many times about how one day when we were older we were going to take sailing lessons so we could pilot our own boat around the world. We both loved the water and we were itching to try our sea legs. I hadn't thought about it in a while with how busy life had been. Yet there before me was a beautiful 60 foot sailing yacht called what else? 'The Brat'.

Adam had done up the deck with heaters and in the center of this was an elegant table set for two. We boarded and were greeted by a serving staff.

"It's what we always talked about. Adam, it is truly breathtaking. Congratulations on the purchase of your first yacht."

"Congratulate us, Montana. It's ours, not mine. I bought it for us. I figured we could take the sailing lessons we talked about and when we are ready for that world tour we'll have some idea what we are doing. This is my gift to us, our weekend toy for when we are home."

We had the most romantic dinner we'd ever had, entirely French. After dinner, he showed me the inside of the yacht. It was even more gorgeous than the outside. Complete with a big room for us and a couple of guest rooms, a living area and a kitchen.

"I'm feeling kind of like getting naked," I said, sprawling on the bed in our room. "Are you ready to christen this huge bed?"

He pulled me to the edge of the bed and slowly unzipped one boot at a time. He peeled off my stockings and undergarments. He kissed the sole of each foot and then started traveling up my legs. I was writhing almost immediately. I felt lost in sensation and the closer he got to the tops of my thighs the more excited I became.

He positioned himself on his elbows and began to swirl his tongue around my clit. I arched my back pressing into his mouth, wanting, needing more. He flipped me over onto my stomach and unzipped my dress, as he pulled it off of me he pulled my hips so my ass was high in the air.

I was so ready, but he was not. Instead of entering me, he pulled me back into him until we were spooning standing up. He reached around with his hands teasing my nipples, his mouth on my ear, continuing his slow seduction and driving me crazy with desire.

He lay me down on my back and tied my hands to the corner posts of the captain's bed. Standing before me he undressed, and once naked climbed onto the bed. He spread my legs wide, bending my knees so my feet were planted.

He clamped his teeth onto my right nipple as he pressed against the opening of my vagina. I moaned and tried to press onto him but I was stuck, immobile. Finally, needing release, I started to beg for him to move inside of me.

When he entered me I climaxed instantly, and was working towards a second climax within seconds. "More," I breathed. "more, don't stop." I gasped as I was thrown into another orgasm. He moved slowly, building now to his own release. I felt him getting close, and pressed against him meeting his thrusts. He exploded and so did I. I could feel the boat rocking with gentle waves, at least some of which we had caused.

He untied me and pulled me into his arms, "Adam, if I ever just want to stay home it will be because I want to do that all day long, every day, forever."

The next morning Adam had me call Ace, Danny and Alex and invite them down to the marina, but not tell them about the boat.

"Dress warmly," I said to Alex, "don't eat, just join us."

"Montana what are you up to now?' Alex asked.

"I'm not telling, just trust me."

The catering company who had done the dinner had already come and cleaned up and reset with breakfast for five. I had a better look at the yacht in the daylight hours, and a perfect view of approaching traffic. When I saw Dan's car pull into the marina, I walked up to meet them as my remarkable brothers disembarked.

"You're not in trouble again, are you?" Ace asked, with a look of concern. "What are we doing here?"

I was so excited I was almost jumping up and down, "Just follow me," I said, and took them down to the wharf where we were anchored.

Alex noticed first, "Holy moly. Guys, will you look at what Adam bought."

The other two looked and their jaws dropped open. Adam stood smiling at the railing.

"Ahoy, welcome to the Brat! Come aboard for some breakfast and a little sail?"

"Hell ya," said Danny, and the guys came aboard.

"Nice digs, Adam. This is pretty spectacular," Ace said, as he examined every detail.

"Come on Ace, sit down. there's time for that later." The five of us sat down to breakfast. When we were done stuffing ourselves, the catering service came and cleaned up while Adam showed the guys the inside.

I could hear them oohing and awing. I stayed on top just to stare out at the ocean and feeling inspired, I wrote a song. By the time the guys came back to the deck I had the song done and I handed it to Alex.

"What is this?"

"Our next hit," I answered. He smiled as he tucked it in his pocket.

The crew was ready so we left on our excursion. Despite being winter weather, and cool, the sky was bright with winter sunshine. We were dressed warmly and of course there were the deck heaters. Adam had already filled our closet with clothing so I was in need of nothing.

I was always in awe of Adam when he did things that required this much thought and I had no clue as to its going on. When could he plan this stuff anyway? All of his time was spent creating, selling, and being with me.

Ace joined me at the rail. "Your boyfriend is something else Mo. He bought himself a beautiful boat."

I smiled, "Yes he did, but it's not his, it's ours. The ownership papers are in both our names." He whistled dramatically and low to indicate how big a deal this was.

"With all these positive things happening for you, I can't think of anyone more deserving."

I smiled but said nothing. The only way it could get better was if there was no fear. Mercy was still out there and I had my nightmares. Maybe, with time, all of that would go away. Somehow, I knew that my journey would be long and filled with many trials.

For a moment I wondered if mom knew. If she knew and had sent me Adam. I hated to think where I would be in life without him.

"Did dad ever think we would do so well?"

His turn to smile, "Yes, we both agreed that the Stanford kids would all do well. We talked about it when he and I first went to the lawyer. He felt that what he had put in place would be enough to sustain us until we made it. I think you and Alex have exceeded anything we could have imagined."

"Ace, what did he say about me, specifically?"

"He said: She is a handful, just like you were. Keep her safe."

"Yep," he responded to my brow raising, "I was the brat until you were born. You took over that nickname right away as far as I was concerned, but to dad you were always his Peanut."

"Did dad like Adam, do you think?"

"Dad thought Adam was totally great, really respected him and his obvious love for you."

"Do you like Adam?" I asked suddenly needing to know that Adam was completely accepted by my surrogate parent.

"I love Adam like a brother."

A wave of relief flooded through me, "I'm so glad. It is so important to me that all of us are close."

We grew silent after that, gazing at the water, each deep in our own thoughts. "How are you, Montana? Just over a week ago someone tried to murder you, how do you feel about that?"

"That is a very good question Ace. I don't know the answer. But if what you want to know is if I'm fragile, about to lose it? No, I'm okay, I feel old, brother, way older than my age. Way beyond, already. And…I do wonder from time to time…if I just wasn't meant for a long life here on earth."

I was surprised by my fessing up to my dark and repetitive thought. I had not shared that with anyone, and the matter of fact way in which I shared it didn't raise alarms in either of us. In response Ace looked thoughtful.

About two hours into our trip the captain parked the yacht at a dock that had stairs that went up to a cliff. "Where are we?" I asked.

"Just past Sechelt," Adam said. "I have something to show you guys." We hopped out of the boat and followed Adam up the stairs to a cliff. The property at the top was gorgeous. "Wow," I said, "Who owns the land?"

"Ace, what do you think of it?" Adam asked him.

"It's beautiful. Is it yours?"

"No. It belongs to all of us, the five of us." He pulled land deeds out of his back pocket. "What you see before you are 10 acres. I purchased this property thinking we could build a family compound with all the works, and then it dawned on me that you each would want your own dwelling also, so I have deeded you each an acre. It has been staked off already and approved for a residential dwelling.

Except you, Montana. You see that decommissioned lighthouse down there? It's on its own three acres and that is just for you. I know you always imagined what it would be like to build a studio in a lighthouse so here it is. I've had my dad's realtors scouting for property with a lighthouse on it since before Dan and I left for Europe."

"This is so much I'm dizzy with it! I wanna see!" And I took off at a run.

"That is how your life is going to be, Adam. Always chasing after that little minx."

"Then I should buy a leash," he said to Ace, and ran after me.

He caught up with me at the stairs to the lighthouse. "Adam, it's like we have come to the end of the earth and hit heaven. This is amazing."

He wrapped his arms around me and held me until our breathing returned to normal. "I might have been standing here alone, thinking of you in heaven had things turned out differently. Your court date is coming up, are you ready for it?"

"Honestly, yes. I feel it is the right thing to do to put those guys away and the risks are known. But I'm terrified for a different reason. This still has not been tied to Mercy. It's bad enough to think that she was behind the original attack, and the last attack. But what if this is completely separate from Mercy and now I have *two* rogue groups trying to off me?

I'm still having nightmares, Adam. They've calmed down for now but if Mercy has her sights on me she will be foiled only so many times. If she hates me so much, she will never stop. Not even you can protect me from everything. There isn't enough money in the world for that much hate." He held me close, rubbing my back, kissing the top of my head as I shuddered, "I saw pictures of some of the other victims, it was bad."

"Well, that's another reason you need a remote place to hide out. We have enough people watching out. This too shall pass, just try not to think about it. Let Eddy, my dad, the cops, and the bodyguards worry about your safety. We've got law enforcement, good and powerful friends, and enough money. All you need to do is live. I won't let anything happen to you."

"I know," I sighed, content for the moment to be in his arms. His strong, athletic painter arms felt so good around me.

The gang was back on the boat and waiting for us when we arrived. We pulled out and headed back. The guys talked about what they wanted to do with their pieces of land and Ace and Adam had a long discussion about the communal area he wanted to build. Ace suggested a resort lodge where people from the city could come to relax when we weren't using it. The ideas just spilled out of me.

"We could use it for fund-raising and we could open it up to families that don't have any money-- and once a month we could host a group. We could offer a week's stay as a big ticket item for other groups as a prize-- and even begin an artists' commune where you and Danny can contribute back. Those things are write-offs aren't they Ace?"

Ace and Adam looked at each other and renewed their conversation about more reasonable possibilities, liability etc. Once docked, Danny and Adam had some pressing engagement so they took off in Adam's car and I went home with Alex and Ace in Dan's.

Over the next few days Alex and Otter and I worked in our garage on the new song I had written on the boat. Alex had taken the lyrics and put the rest of it together and it sounded really hot, really upbeat. It was nice to play in our garage. I had nothing else to do anyway, with Danny, Ace and Adam busy working.

Much to our surprise, Otter wrote his first song and it was good so we worked on that one right up until it was time for us to head to Victoria for Christmas. We spent five glorious days in Victoria harbour in a gorgeous Penthouse with our families there for the big day.

The highlight for me was when Otter's mom looked out the window at his prompting. Way down below sat a new BMW with a big red bow. A Christmas gift from her son. She was in tears and Otter choked up. It was wonderful to see him so happy to give her the car.

Adam's parents handed him a manila envelope. Inside was a picture and specs for a condo/apartment three blocks away from my house downtown. A five bedroom penthouse with a limited view of the water, "What's this?" he asked, glancing from his mom to his dad for an explanation.

"Son, we thought it was time for you to move out from above the garage to your own place. So, we bought you a penthouse in the West End. It's newly renovated, and although it's only a midrise, you can--"

"--Adam, go and thank your parents!" I was more excited than he was. He was in shock.

"I... don't know what to say," he finally managed. "This is incredible. Thank you seems so inadequate," he finished, hugging them tightly. We'd always kept our activities fairly quiet at his place due to the close proximity to his parents. What adventures we might have in this place I could only imagine.

Chapter 11

The Christmas season had been great and with the new year the band and the artists were back in our busy groove. Adam and I had time between boxing day and the new year to check out his new penthouse.

The elevator sported a polished brass door and opened up right into his penthouse. Apartment was almost a misnomer the place was so huge. It wasn't just the five bedrooms with two regular bathrooms off the hallways, it had a grand foyer with a piano, a massive kitchen and large dining space with bay windows and a large living room with decks out either end. We could easily entertain 50 people in his new pad.

The master suite was enormous and had an ensuite with a sunken soaker tub for two. One of the bedrooms on the south east side had sunshine for most of the day so he decided to make that one of two studios, the other he put into a north west room where the light stayed constant all day and it wouldn't get too hot in the summer. The other two bedrooms would be for guests.

Adam moved in the week after New Year's. He painted it to his liking and then we shopped. That was the best part. He wanted a combination of antiques and modern so we went to auctions, high end stores, you name it. In the living room he put a huge screen projection TV down one end and he bought two leather sofas angled for conversation around a massive coffee table. Two reclining leather chairs directly faced the screen.

He ended up spending $50,000.00 on new furniture. Of course, the walls were adorned with his work-- most of which was of me or scenes from my life. He also had some of my photos framed and hanging in various places. I brought over the statue that I had purchased at the art show and he put it on the piano, which was the only furniture in the foyer along with a French style divan.

Adam asked me to move in with him and of course my answer was a resounding yes. My first weekend off I packed and moved into Adam's. I wasn't bringing any furniture, just me and my personal belongings so it was a small move.

Danny and Ace stood at the door, hands in their pockets, looking like lost puppies. "Come on you guys, cheer up! I'm only three blocks away, it's not the end of the world." I gave them each a hug and a kiss. "Don't forget about the dinner party on Friday night."

Alex and I would still be carpooling every morning. We would be together all day long, so for us nothing was changing. I didn't see Ace and Dan often as it was. I was really quiet while Adam and I unloaded and took everything upstairs. Adam kept up the chatter to keep my mind occupied and when we were done, we sat down and had some tea on the patio. It was an incredible spot, absolutely beautiful!

"Montana are you sure you want to be here with me?"

"Adam, there is nothing I want more. In truth I feel so guilty. Did you see those long faces? I feel terrible. I guess one chapter has closed in my life and another has begun. I feel so old, so much older than almost eighteen,. I think this is just the growing pains, you know, cutting the strings and being independent."

The next morning, Alex came over for coffee and breakfast before we headed out. "How is the new pad?" he asked.

"It's fine." I replied.

"I felt weird all night, like I was having an anxiety attack. Was that you?"

"Yes, it was me. I guess I can't hide anything from you," I sighed.

"What's up?"

"I don't know what is up. I just feel sad," and I quickly wiped a tear that had escaped. He didn't say anything, he didn't have to. In our quiet connection we shared everything whether we wanted to or not. Sometimes things got too busy to notice, but recently life had been unusually calm.

Alex dropped me off after work. He declined my invite to come up. When I entered the penthouse I found a note from Adam addressed to Anne Hathaway (*Shakespeare's wife, not the Hollywood star to be decades later). 'My dearest Anne, I will be home promptly at 6:00 pm. I would like a dinner with all the trimmings, my slippers at the ready and my glass of red wine poured. Love Will, P.S. Just kidding bringing home sushi see you at 6:00.'

I had an hour so I decided to play a game. I showered and changed and wrote him a note of clues to my hiding spot and at 5:55 I hid. Precisely at 6:00 I heard the elevator open. A moment later I heard him call out; "Oh Anne, is dinner ready?"

N.M McGregor

Then silence as he read my note and looked over the clues; I did my best to keep from laughing every time I heard him walk by me and he didn't look up. Finally after half an hour he said, "I give up, you'd better come out. The sushi will go bad." I lost it and lay there laughing. I heard him below me say, "Okay, I'm lying. I put it in the fridge. I can hear you, where are you?"

That started a fresh peal of laughter from me and I heard him below me moving stuff around and then he pushed up the roof tile, "You sneaky thing," he said, "good spot." He moved out of the way so I could climb down and he gave me a long kiss. He grabbed a bottle and two wine glasses in the kitchen. "Come see where we're going to eat," he said, leading me to the sliding doors that opened onto the deck.

"Outside? Are you crazy, mister?" We went out into a brisk evening. The place had come with amazing heaters that were like the ones they have on patios at restaurants so despite the cold weather, we were warm enough at the table. We drank wine and talked about our day.

"How did it go today?" he asked.

"Good." I said, "We are rehearsing that new song that I wrote on the yacht on our first time out."

"Really? What's it about?"

"Let me grab it for you and you can read it." I brought it out to him and he read it silently to himself. He sucked in his breath in a soft whistle and said, "Sing it, Mo. Sing it for me."

I went beet red. I couldn't say that I couldn't do it, he knew better. He'd heard me sing in the shower and I often mouthed the words along with Alex when we performed. "Okay," I said, and closed my eyes and drew in a big breath, letting it out slowly. I wavered in the first stanza, but I drew in my focus and sank my teeth into the song, just like I would playing drums. I allowed myself to be carried away and before I knew it, I was done.

N.M McGregor

I could feel him staring at me but I didn't want to open my eyes. I was terrified that the gaze would be one of disapproval. I felt a hand on my cheek caressing my skin. I opened my eyes to find Adam gazing at me, his eyes glistening and filled with love.

"Thank you, he said, "that was beautiful." Sushi forgotten, I moved closer and straddled him on his chair. We kissed passionately. Moments later we were removing each other's clothing as we moved inside. Two hours later, we finally had our wine and dinner and I was feeling better about where I was....

Friday night we set up the dinner party on the deck. We had the heaters and patio lanterns on. Champagne was chilling, appetizers ready. With coolers of beer, we made it look like a beach party. Dan and Alex got there right on time and I gave them a tour.

Ace and Kristine arrived a short time later and Adam gave them the tour while I made the drinks. After dinner Ace stood and said he had news. We

398

waited expectantly. "Now that I have your attention-"

This was too much for me, "Yes, yes, get on with it man!"

"Very well. I asked Kristine to marry me and she said yes."

I was just taking a sip of champagne and choked on it. "What did you just say?" No one heard me. They were all congratulating Ace and Kristine. I stood up to add my congratulations and gave them hugs and looked happy for them. In truth, I felt wooden. The gap I had been feeling between Ace and me since walking out the front door of the house widened and became a valley.

Ace said that they were going to wait until next year so Kristine would be fully graduated and working in her field. He and Kristine would live in the house until they decided where they wanted to go. I was trying not to be weird but I was in shock at the news. He had said he wouldn't get married until he was 30!

Later, after everyone had left Adam and I were cleaning up. "1 guess that was a bit of a shock," he said.

"What do you mean?" I tried to be coy.

"You've been a zombie since dinner. It seems like Ace's announcement really threw you." I didn't say anything. I could feel myself retreating and I didn't know what to do about it. I knew I wasn't being rational. I was being stupid, but my feelings said my dad was leaving me, because that was really what Ace was to me. To both Alex and me. Alex had been unusually quiet after dinner so I knew he was feeling the same. It was too much at once and I was disappearing under the change and pressure.

"Montana." I didn't answer, I just kept picking up dishes. "Montana, look at me." I looked him in the eyes and I can only guess that my expression matched my inner turmoil. He took the dishes out of my hands and led me into the living room. He sat me down and talked quietly in my ear, "It's okay, Mo. It's going to be okay. Hang in there, kiddo. You're doing great." That's when the floodgates opened and I cried like a baby and then somewhat more like an adult as I calmed down. Then it started over. It seemed like hours and I still felt so much remorse and confusion.

I vaguely remember Adam putting me to bed. I woke feeling groggy, glancing over to the clock, it was 1:17pm. I was surprised to see that I had slept so late.

"Adam," I called, no answer. Hmm, he must have had some errands to run. I threw on a t-shirt and a pair of shorts and made my way to the kitchen to get some coffee. I caught a masculine back out of the corner of my eye sitting at the kitchen table, "There you are," I said.

When he turned around I saw it wasn't Adam, it was Ace. "Oh hey, Ace what are you doing here?

Where is Adam?" I grabbed a cup of coffee and sat down opposite him.

"Danny and Adam had some meetings today and won't be back until later, so you're stuck with me." He was staring straight through me. It gave me a very uncomfortable feeling. The way he and Adam could do that always made me feel stupid and immature. I had no idea why, it just did.

"Tell me what is going on Montana, right now."

"I don't know what you're talking about Ace, there is nothing going on."

"Adam says there is."

"Well, Adam is lying."

"Montana Stanford, Adam doesn't lie. But you... are notorious for it, and I am not leaving until you spill. Speak or I will blister your butt." That infuriated me.

"You will do no such thing. This is my bloody house."

He stood and scooped me up and over his shoulder and headed for the couch. "I certainly can and I will unless you smarten up and tell your big brother exactly what is going on with you."

"Put me down you bully." I was hammering on his back and kicking my legs. "You put me down this instant, Ace Stanford."

I was over his lap. "Wait!" I cried. One large well-muscled hand swatted my right butt cheek, "Wait for what? Are you going to spill?"

"I feel like you have shut me out and replaced me with Kristine," I said quietly. He sat me up and two silent tears escaped down my cheeks. "I feel like this is some twisted punishment for moving out, that you are angry with me."

"Oh Peanut," he said, pulling me in for a tight hug. "How could I possibly replace you?"

"You always said you wouldn't get married until you were 30. You're only 25. I'm not prepared. I'm not ready to lose you. You're leaving me behind, just like mom and dad. You promised I wouldn't get lost."

I started to hyperventilate. Images played through my inner vision just like the day I tried to drown myself. I started to shake. The images were becoming more violent. I started to panic.

"I…can't…breathe…."I wheezed. Ace ran to the kitchen and grabbed a paper bag. Holding it over my face, he told me to breathe. When that didn't work he gently held my head down between my knees. I stopped spiraling. My breath stabilized and so did my vision. I sat up. He gave me a glass of whiskey. "Drink." I pushed it away.

"This didn't work last time..."

"Fair enough." Ace placed the glass on the coffee table. "Montana, you have Adam. You are taken care of. I will always be your brother and guardian. Nothing will ever change that and I will always be here for you. There are no guarantees in life. You need to learn to be okay without them.. I would like to say that Kristine and I will live happily ever after, but who knows?

I sometimes wish that you hadn't found your true love so young but you did. He will be there for you and can provide for you in every way. Focus on moving forward. Don't live in the past, don't let it hold you back."

The elevator opened and the guys strolled in. I must have looked like hell, but nothing they all hadn't seen before. Ace stood up and went out onto the deck to talk to Adam. Danny grabbed a beer and sat down beside me.

"You look like you have had a rough day," he commented casually. I didn't respond.

"Did Ace help you work out your stuff?"

"I'm sure he will tell you all about it on the way home." I rolled my eyes sarcastically.

"Did you want to tell me your version?" he asked.

I looked out the window. They were still deep in chat mode out there.

"Danny I don't think I can handle life. It is too big and I feel like I'm being swallowed up." He gave me a searching look and nodded his head," I feel that way sometimes too. Adam keeps me grounded when I start to feel overwhelmed. That is why the lure of the drugs was so strong, it took away the panic. Overnight success is really intimidating. I think Adam is so good at it because he was groomed right from the start for success. I feel like I don't deserve it and without Adam I would be nothing."

Wow, this was a huge revelation. Danny had never talked about his feelings with me. He looked so forlorn, and I got it that it wasn't just me. It was all of us and we needed to stick together no matter where our paths took us.

"Do you think Ace ever feels the same way as us?"

"Oh, I know he does. I have seen him cry and get scared more times than you can possibly imagine. He needs someone other than us. We are his responsibilities and he will always feel that way. He needs someone who fills that gap for him, just like Adam does for you." Danny's words cut through my brain fog. He made it so clear, I was an idiot.

"Dan you're a genius!"

"I am?"

"Out of every person I have ever met, you say the most with the least amount of words. I couldn't see his perspective, I could only see my own. Thank you for showing me that I have been a selfish baby. He needs her. That makes sense to me, and as long as he still loves us and we get some time together I'm happy. Thanks Dan the Man."

I joined the guys on the deck with a poker face. Adam and Ace turned to watch my approach. They looked guarded. They probably thought I was going to jump. A big grin spread across my face. I pulled

Ace in for a hug.

"I get it, you just need someone for your own who can fill in all those needs that you have that you can't get from us. I am your responsibility and will always be, and all you have been trying to do is have something for your own. I'm a bonehead, and I am sorry."

He smiled and hugged me back hard. The three of us went inside and had some drinks and ordered in some food. The rest of our evening was spent telling jokes and funny stories. In that moment we were all fine. Wherever our paths took us, I knew we would always be there for each other.

It was our eighteenth birthday. We were having a celebration at the Penthouse, a catered affair with tons of booze. Alex and Allyson were first to arrive. They purchased a Penthouse across the street from us, directly opposite ours. We could wave to each other from our balconies, our walkie talkies were in range and we had fun with that. "Roger. Coffee at 0600. Over and out." It was fun.

Ace and Kristine arrived next and I gave her a proper welcome to the family along with an apology for the other night. Kristine was very understanding, she had been around awhile and had seen me through a few of my previous meltdowns.

Danny showed up dateless again. Otter and Tim brought Ann and Stella. Most surprisingly Chrissie arrived with Eddy. Throughout the evening various people popped in. Alex and I had a blast.

With all the comings and goings, the penthouse elevator never stopped. It wasn't until almost everyone had left and nearly daylight that I saw a present on the piano. Adam was saying goodbye at the elevator to Alex and Allyson, who were the last to leave.

I picked up the present and gave it a little shake. Whatever was inside was awfully light. I opened it and inside was a picture. A picture of little me, maybe 7 or 8, tied up with a gag in my mouth. Across the photo in red marker were the words,

"YOUR ASS IS MINE LITTLE BITCH. I WILL FINISH WHAT I STARTED."

I promptly passed out.

Like to Read for Free?

West End Montana

1st in the Montana Series, is now free on all major platforms

Check out www.nmmcgregor.com

Sign up for your free copy of West End Brat

2nd in the Montana Series

Have you Read?

West End Montana:

Meet Montana Stanford, a precocious teen with an iron will and a passion for life that affects everyone around her. Living with her brothers in Vancouver's West End, she seeks love and excitement in everything she does. Of course, life is no bed of roses as she attracts the ire of some easy opponents and makes some enemies who are harder to shake.

https://books2read.com/westendmontana

West End Brat:

Montana has finally found her true love, but will her past destroy their future?

Her life could be described as tumultuous. Every step forward is followed by three steps back until she starts dating philanthropist, Adam Northrop. With him at her side, navigating the unchartered waters of her blooming career seems easy. Until her world begins to unravel. A malevolent plot is brought to light, one intended to end her career and possibly her life.

If you like The Girl Who Lived, The Billionaire Collection, A little bird Told me, or Dreams of Orchids, then get ready for a whole new adventure with The Montana Series.

https://books2read.com/book2westendbrat

Moon Goddess Chronicles

Petals of Awakening 1st Book in the series

Petals of Awakening:

A week-long trip is just what she needs, little does Mary know the shockwaves that come from her excursion will be life threatening!

Mary has been trapped as a plaything for too long. She is lost and in need of help to move forward. Wealthy and single George Clooney look alike, Edward Stanhope likes Mary exactly where she is and wants to keep her there. Tension builds between the two until one is left standing, who will it be?

If you liked Gone Girl, Lie To me or Girl on the Train you will love N.M. McGregor's new Petals of Awakening.

https://books2read.com/petals

Enjoy this book?

You can make a difference.

Reviews are the most powerful tools when it comes to getting my books recognized.

I am not in the financial position to place full page ads like large publishing houses do, at least not yet.

What I do have is something far more powerful.

A group of committed and loyal followers!

Reviews of my books help to bring them to the attention of other readers.

If you enjoyed this book, I would be grateful if you could take 5 minutes and leave a review on Amazon.

HTTPS://BOOKS2READ.COM/BOOK2WESTENDBRAT

ACKNOWLEDGMENTS

Thanks to my West End Tribe. You created a vibrant backdrop from which to process my creativity.

Thank you to my editor and book cover designer Drew Taylor. My writing is better because of your intervention and encouragement to be better at my craft.

A huge thanks to my husband and children for their belief in me and support through the writing process.

To my technical support Jen Eaton. I couldn't have done any of it without you.

To my supporters, THANK YOU! Without you, who would read my stories? Thank you for your ongoing support and encouragement.

Made in the USA
San Bernardino, CA
21 December 2018